SPARK STUDENT MOTIVATION

101 Easy Activities for Cooperative Learning

JOLENE L. ROEHLKEPARTAIN

SEARCH
INSTITUTE
PRESS

Spark Student Motivation:
101 Easy Activities for Cooperative Learning
by Jolene L. Roehlkepartain

The following are registered trademarks of Search Institute: Search Institute®, Developmental Assets®, and Healthy Communities • Healthy Youth®.

Search Institute Press, Minneapolis, MN
Copyright © 2012 by Search Institute

At the time of publication, all facts and figures cited herein are the most current available; all telephone numbers, addresses, and website URLs are accurate and active; all publications, organizations, websites, and other resources exist as described in this book; and all efforts have been made to verify them. The author and Search Institute make no warranty or guarantee concerning the information and materials given out by organizations or content found at websites that are cited herein, and we are not responsible for any changes that occur after this book's publication. If you find an error or believe that a resource listed herein is not as described, please contact Client Services at Search Institute.

10 9 8 7 6 5 4 3 2 1

Printed on acid-free paper in the United States of America.

Search Institute
615 First Avenue Northeast, Suite 125
Minneapolis, MN 55413
612-376-8955 • 877-240-7251, ext. 1
www.search-institute.org

ISBN-13: 978-1-57482-494-0

Credits
Editors: Rebecca Post and Catherine L. Broberg
Book Design: Kinne Design
Production Supervisor: Mary Ellen Buscher

Library of Congress
Cataloging-in-Publication Data
Roehlkepartain, Jolene L.
    Spark student motivation : 101 easy activities for cooperative learning / by Jolene L. Roehlkepartain.
    p. cm.
Includes index.
ISBN-13: 978-1-57482-494-0 (pbk.)
ISBN-10: 1-57482-494-5 (pbk.)
1. Education, Elementary—Activity programs.
2. Group work in education. 3. Motivation in education. I. Title.

LB1592.R635 2012
372.13—dc23
                                        2011041923

Licensing and Copyright

CONTENTS

Working More Effectively with Groups of Kids

Whenever I work with a group of fourth, fifth, or sixth graders, I always have high hopes before the group starts. I can envision the group working well together, individuals succeeding, and group members getting along.

Then the group starts, and I discover a different reality. Many don't want to be there. Their parents signed them up and made them go. Some are more interested in talking with their friends than doing anything else. Some think *everything* we do is boring.

Yet whenever I take a different approach and ignite the sparks of young people, they get excited to participate.

What are sparks? Sparks are interests, talents, and passions. A spark is something that gives each person (whether a child, a teen, or an adult) meaning and purpose in life.

What kind of sparks do fourth to sixth graders have? Some love to play a musical instrument. Others can't wait to get outside and kick around a soccer ball. Some get excited about role-playing video games. Others care deeply about animals and are always finding animals to help and care for.

Search Institute researchers have identified more than 200 sparks. (View the list at www.ignitesparks.org/sparks_list.html.) As we help young people find their sparks (and the groups we work with identify their group spark), we can lead, coach, and teach more effective groups.

By taking a spark approach to your group, you can help kids become more successful. You can connect kids with what they are passionate about, and you can unlock the outcomes you want.

Critical Outcomes

Which outcomes are most critical for a group? You want kids engaged in your program (class, club, or team). You want them excited to attend. You want them to get to know the other group members and build deeper relationships. You want the group—and each individual—to succeed.

Yet, too often we focus solely on the outcomes we want—or the outcomes handed to us. Teachers have academic goals to reach. Coaches want to win games. Music teachers want their students to master an instrument. Club leaders want kids to work together to earn a scout badge or accomplish a service project or some other type of project.

These outcomes are important, but it's difficult to achieve these outcomes when we neglect the essential group process outcomes that can get us there. That's what this book is about: accomplishing vital group process outcomes so that you can reach the other outcomes you want.

Engaging a Diversity of Young People

In effective education, using differentiated instruction and doing activities that tap into the eight multiple intelligences, are some of the key ways to keep kids engaged and curious. The activities in this book also encompass these two learning theories.

Howard Gardner, author of *Multiple Intelligences: New Horizons in Theory and Practice,* has identified eight different ways to present information so that all young people assimilate that information. Here are the eight multiple intelligences Gardner identified:

- words (linguistic intelligence)
- numbers or logic (logical-mathematical intelligence)
- pictures (spatial intelligence)
- music (musical intelligence)
- self-reflection (intrapersonal intelligence)
- physical experiences (bodily-kinesthetic intelligence)
- social (interpersonal intelligence)
- natural world experiences (naturalist intelligence)

Search Institute has taken the more than 200 sparks it has identified and placed them into 29 major spark categories. If you examine these 29 major spark categories with the eight multiple intelligences, you discover that these 29 major spark categories fit into all eight multiple intelligences. See the chart, "Sparks and Multiple Intelligences" on page four.

Carol Tomlinson's groundbreaking work on differentiated instruction also fits well with the theory of multiple intelligence and with sparks. Her most recent book, *Managing a Differentiated Classroom* (New York: Scholastic Teaching Resources, 2011), focuses on making and managing groups, which is a key element to an effective classroom, athletic team, club, or any other type of group.

One of the biggest challenges for group leaders and teachers is group or classroom management. More and more kids are acting out, and many have not developed the social skills to be effective group members. While decreasing disruptive behavior is a key goal, it's also essential to promote positive social skills among all group members.

Child Trends, a national nonprofit research center that focuses on improving the lives of children and families, recently reviewed 38 rigorously evaluated programs to identify what was effective in teaching young people positive social skills.[1] Child Trend researchers found the following effective elements

- doing peer-related activities
- creating working pairs
- developing peer teaching
- employing multiple instruction strategies (in other words: multiple intelligence)
- using technology[2]

These key elements are incorporated in the activities of this book.

---

1. Tawana Bandy and Kristin Moore, "What Works for Promoting and Enhancing Positive Social Skills," *Child Trends Fact Sheet,* Publication #2011-07, March 2011.

2. Ibid.

Sparks and Multiple Intelligences

Search Institute has identified 29 major spark categories. Here's how they fit in with the eight multiple intelligences identified by Howard Gardner.

Words LINGUISTIC INTELLIGENCE	Numbers or Logic LOGICAL-MATHEMATICAL INTELLIGENCE	Pictures SPATIAL INTELLIGENCE	Music MUSICAL INTELLIGENCE
• Journalism spark • Leadership spark • Learning spark • Reading spark • Speech spark • Teaching and coaching spark • Writing spark	• Building and design spark • Computers spark • Engineering spark • Entrepreneurship spark • Leadership spark • Learning spark • Teaching and coaching spark	• Creative arts spark • Leadership spark • Learning spark • Photography, film spark • Teaching and coaching spark • Visual arts spark	• Leadership spark • Learning spark • Music spark • Teaching and coaching spark

Self-Reflection INTRAPERSONAL INTELLIGENCE	Physical Experiences BODILY-KINESTHETIC INTELLIGENCE	Social INTERPERSONAL INTELLIGENCE	Natural World Experiences NATURALIST INTELLIGENCE
• Leadership spark • Learning spark • Living in a specific way spark • Spirituality spark • Teaching and coaching spark	• Dance, movement spark • Drama, theater spark • Learning spark • Leadership spark • Sports, athletic spark • Teaching and coaching spark	• Advocacy spark • Comedy spark • Family spark • Leadership spark • Learning spark • Relationships spark • Serving, helping, volunteering spark • Solving social problems spark • Speech spark • Teaching and coaching spark	• Advocacy spark • Animals spark • Leadership spark • Learning spark • Living in a specific way spark • Nature, ecology, environment spark • Outdoor life spark • Serving, helping, volunteering spark • Solving social problems spark • Teaching and coaching spark

Note: Some sparks appear in more than one intelligence area.

How to Use This Book

Most of the activities in this book can be completed in less than 15 minutes, with some chapters focusing on quick, easy activities that can be done in 1 to 3 minutes. (You also can find some longer activities that encourage young people to create or build in a new way.) Use activities in whatever ways best fit your needs. Consider these possibilities:

Create an overall strategy that incorporates these activities. What do you wish to accomplish from a group-process perspective? Do you want young people to get to know each other's names? (See activities in chapter 1: Greeting Activities.) Do you want young people to follow the rules? (See activities in chapter 2: Creating Rules and Routine Activities.) Do you want to help young people identify their sparks? (See activities in chapter 8: Helping Kids Find Their Sparks Activities.)

Choose individual activities. Find specific activities that fit into your ongoing plans for your group. Integrate these activities into your existing curriculum, group objectives, group outcomes, or group plans. Find activities through the chapter headings or through the two indices at the end of the book (a topical index and a spark index).

Focus on a theme area. As you gather as a group, you may discover that your group isn't working well together. Choose activities that focus on changing that. Activities in chapters 4 and 5, Community-Building Activities and Acting-Together Activities, will be helpful.

Create a notebook of all the ready-to-use handouts. This book includes 24 ready-to-use handouts. Each of the eight chapters closes with three handouts. Consider creating a notebook of these handouts for each group member, and have them decorate a cover for their notebooks and write their names on them. Then periodically have young people do a handout activity. Be sure to collect the notebooks at the end of each session to ensure that all young people will have their notebooks during the next group time. At your last session, return the notebooks to the young people to take home.

Combine several activities into one session. Some leaders have taken one activity from each of the eight chapters and used them in one session to emphasize how important each outcome (getting to know one another from the greeting activities in chapter 1 and working independently from the activities in chapter 6) is. Others have used a number of activities when their group gathers for a retreat or a longer event.

Use activities to connect young people with adults. Young people flourish with their sparks when they get to know adults who are interested in them and their sparks. In his book, *Sparks: How Parents Can Help Ignite the Hidden Strengths of Teenagers,* Peter Benson advocates that young people need key adults in their lives to support, nourish, and guide their sparks.

Help young people create an individual sparks notebook. Every young person has at least one spark. Some of your young people will be able to identify their spark (or sparks) with ease. Others will be stumped. Have each young person create a sparks notebook. Use the activities in this book to help them discover new sparks, deepen the sparks they already have, and find ways to connect with others who can support them on their spark journey.

Keep talking. Each activity in this book includes a list of questions to debrief the activity. These discussion questions are based on the service-learning discussion model of reflecting on *what* (what happened?), *so what* (why is this important?), and *now what* (what can we do next?).

Have high expectations. Don't let your group become stagnant. Deal with issues as they arise. If young people aren't following the rules, dive into the activities of chapter 2 (Creating Rules and Routines Activities). If they're forming cliques, focus on the activities in chapter 3 (Sharing Activities) and chapter 4 (Community-Building Activities). Hold high expectations for your group and each individual in your group. You'll notice a difference.

Expect setbacks. I once led a group of sixth-grade boys that ended in a complete disaster. I was so focused on trying to get them to learn and master a musical piece that I didn't work on helping the group to gel. In hindsight, I realized I made some key errors. These boys really liked each other and didn't have enough time to enjoy being together. I hadn't included them in setting rules and routines (thus they didn't buy in to my rules). I hadn't helped them to find their sparks.

Yet, I learned from this difficult experience. Since then, I've led a number of successful groups of upper-elementary kids. I now tap into their curiosity, their interests, and the relationships they already have. I start with what's working in parts of the group and expand those strengths to the entire group.

That's why I wrote this book. It's my guidebook for getting groups of young people to work together well.

Who Can Use This Book?

Anyone who works with students in grades 4–6 can benefit from the creative activities in this book—whether you're in a school, an after-school program, a youth program, a faith-based program, a club, an athletic team, an arts group, a recreational program, or a community-based program.

Because this book appeals to a broad audience, we have chosen language that will be understood by diverse group leaders. As you read this book, you may want to customize the language or the activities to fit your specific goals.

The activities are designed to be used with young people in grades 4–6. Depending on the maturity, interest, and skill level of your group members, you may discover that some activities are more appropriate for grades 4 or 5 while others are more appropriate for grades 5 or 6. (Young people go through a lot of changes between grades 4 and 6.) Adapt activities to best fit your needs.

In addition, the following activities can easily be adapted for teenagers: 1–2, 4, 7, 10–13, 14–16, 18–19, 22, 25–28, 31, 34–36, 38, 40–41, 45–49, 51–53, 57, 59–60, 62–63, 65–66, 69–71, 73–74, 76, 78, 80, 83–86, 88–94, 96–101.

How This Book Is Organized

Whether a leader (teacher, coach, or volunteer) is working with fourth- to sixth-graders in a youth program, classroom, club, sport, or some other type of endeavor, there are certain activities that all effective leaders (or teachers) do:

- They're intentional with how they greet young people, and they create ways for young people to greet each other in positive ways. See chapter 1: Greeting Activities.

- They create rules and routines so everyone knows what's expected (and how to manage the classroom/activity). See chapter 2: Creating Rules and Routines Activities.

- They develop activities for young people to get to know each other. See chapter 3: Sharing Activities.

- They do community-building (or team-building) activities to create a sense of community and cohesiveness. See chapter 4: Community-Building Activities.

- They do group activities where young people act together as a single group. This ties into the multiple intelligence/learning style of interpersonal intelligence. See chapter 5: Acting-Together Activities.

- They do activities that encourage young people to work independently and become more self-aware. This ties into the multiple intelligence/learning style of intrapersonal intelligence. See chapter 6: Working Independently Activities.

- They do activities that get young people energized and refocused when they start to get bored. Some leaders call these their "bag of tricks." See chapter 7: Breaking-Up-Boredom Activities.

- They do activities to help young people identify their sparks. See chapter 8: Helping Kids Find Their Sparks Activities.

Many classroom teachers of this age group have a "morning meeting," which includes many of the elements from this book. The bestselling book, *The Morning Meeting Book,* by Roxann Kriete (Turners Falls, MA: Northeast Foundation for Children, 2002), makes the case that successful leaders and teachers are intentional with their greeting, setting rules, creating relationship-building activities, and building community.

Effective leaders of programs and clubs for upper-elementary young people are also aware of group dynamics. They help young people get to know each other. They set and enforce rules. They create ways for young people to work together.

By igniting young people's sparks, program leaders and teachers can make their programs (and classrooms) even more effective—and also get kids excited to participate.

Recently, I led an art group of fifth and sixth graders. You could tell who wanted to be there. They were excited and engaged. They were the ones who had convinced their parents to let them participate in this group. You could also easily tell who didn't want to be there: kids whose parents signed them up so they would do something other than play video games all day (which is all they talked about).

We started with a greeting activity from chapter 1, helping the kids get to know each other's name and greet each other. Then we created some rules from chapter 2. Then I jumped into an activity from chapter 8 about helping kids find sparks. I wanted those kids who felt pressured to come to find a connection to our group.

And that worked. We then jumped into the purpose of our group: making art. Those who had willingly signed up jumped right in. They were engaged and couldn't wait to make art. By this time, the reluctant group members were also excited. They were going to make art based on their favorite video game.

Soon the group was buzzing with activity and conversation. One child was having a hard time, so I spent some one-on-one time with that young person. That seemed to help him settle into the art project.

After a while, a few got antsy, but that was easily addressed. I stopped the art activity and did a boredom buster from chapter 7. After getting their wiggles out, the young people went back to creating art.

When our time was over, most enthusiastically greeted their parent(s) or guardian(s), showing them what they had created and describing why they wanted to come back.

Nothing could make me prouder as a group leader.

CHAPTER 1

Greeting Activities

The way you greet kids when they come to your class or activity makes a big difference in setting the tone for your time together. When kids are noticed and feel that their presence matters, they're more likely to engage in all your activities. When you plan a greeting activity for your group to do at the beginning of your time together, kids can get to know each other, learn each other's names, and feel like your group is exactly where they belong. ▶▶

An Alphabet Hello

FOCUS
Kids greet each other by learning each other's names in alphabetical order.

SPARKS TIE-IN
- Learning
- Dance/movement

YOU WILL NEED
- Nothing

ACTIVITY Have young people mingle and create a line where they are in alphabetical order by first name. This may take a while if young people don't know each other. Eventually, they should arrange themselves in alphabetical order, such as Anjali, Brian, Craig, DeAnne, Emily, Franco, and so on.

Once young people are in alphabetical order, form a circle from the line so that everyone is still in alphabetical order. Now the person whose name is at the end of the alphabet will be next to the person whose name is at the beginning of the alphabet; for instance, Zach will be next to Anjali.

Have young people go around in a circle and introduce themselves. Start with the person at the beginning of the alphabet. For example, Anjali says, "Hi Brian. I am Anjali." Brian then turns to the person next to him and says, "Hi Craig. I am Brian." Continue around the circle. If someone doesn't know the name of the person next to him or her, have that person just ask and then do the greeting.

Once you finish, go around the circle in the opposite direction. This allows young people to greet the person on the other side of them.

DISCUSSION QUESTIONS
- What was it like to try to create a line in alphabetical order by first name?
- How do you feel when someone calls you by name? Why?
- Why does it matter how we greet each other?
- How else can we get to know other people's names?

BONUS IDEA Do the activity according to last name.

Hello Around the World

FOCUS
Kids greet each other by saying hello in different languages.

SPARKS TIE-IN
- Learning
- Relationships

YOU WILL NEED
- Nothing

ACTIVITY Have young people sit in a circle. Teach them how to say hello in another language. Some examples include Arabic: "Al Salaam a'alaykum" (pronounced Ahl sah-lahm ah ah-lay-koom), French: "Bonjour" (pronounced Bonn-joor), German: "Guten Tag" (pronounced Goo-ten tahk), Hebrew: "Shalom" (pronounced Shaw-loam), Hindi: "Namaste" (Nah-mah-stay), Japanese: "Konnichiwa" (pronounced Kon-knee-chee-wah), Mandarin: "Ni Hao" (pronounced Knee how), Russian: "Zdraustvuite" (pronounced Zzdrast-voight-yah), Spanish: "Hola" (pronounced Oh-la), and Swahili: "Jambo" (pronounced Jam-bow).

Once young people know the greeting, such as the Swahili "Jambo" pronunciation, point to one person in the circle and have the group say "Jambo Julio" (if the person's name is Julio). Continue around the circle until the group has personally said hello to each person using the non-English greeting and the young person's name.

DISCUSSION QUESTIONS
- What was it like to learn how to say hello in another language?
- How do you feel when we greet you in another language? Why?
- Why does it matter to learn about other languages?
- How else can we greet each other?

BONUS IDEA Ask if anyone in your group knows how to say hello in another language. Have that child teach your group. (This is a great way to affirm a child's cultural heritage.)

Clap, Clap Greeting

FOCUS

Young people greet each other in rhythm.

SPARKS TIE-IN

- Music
- Dance/movement

YOU WILL NEED

- Nothing

ACTIVITY Have young people sit in a circle with you. (They can sit either in chairs or on the floor.) Teach them this rhythm in a steady beat that isn't too fast: with both hands pat your legs twice followed by two claps. Have kids continue to repeat this rhythm.

Once young people know the rhythm, explain that you're going to start this greeting. Everyone will do the rhythm one time. Then on the second time, you will name the person sitting on your left during the first clap and the name of the next person on your left during the second clap. (Demonstrate how this works.) Once they understand, explain that you'll go around the circle clockwise. Each person who is "it" will say the name of the person sitting on his or her left during the first clap and the name of the second person from his or her left during the second clap. Only the person who is "it" will speak, but everyone else will continue the rhythm.

Go around the entire circle until everyone has had a turn.

DISCUSSION QUESTIONS

- What was it like to keep a steady rhythm?
- How did you feel when it was your turn to speak?
- Why greet each other in rhythm when we could just say hello?
- What other rhythms could we use to greet each other?

BONUS IDEA Speed up the rhythm and see how fast young people can do this without making a mistake. Or consider going around the circle counterclockwise after you've completed the circle clockwise.

Sing Your Name

FOCUS
Kids greet each other by singing their name in an unusual way.

SPARKS TIE-IN
- Comedy
- Music

YOU WILL NEED
- Nothing

ACTIVITY Have young people sit in a circle with you. (They can sit either in chairs or on the floor.) Explain that the group members are going to take turns singing their name in whatever way they wish. They can sing it in a funny way, in a soft way, in a loud way, in a crazy way. Give time for young people to think of how they will sing, "I am Kira" (or whatever their first name is).

Ask for a volunteer to start the singing greeting. Then go around the circle clockwise. Continue until everyone has had a turn.

DISCUSSION QUESTIONS
- What was it like to think up an unusual way to sing your name?
- How did you feel when it was your turn to sing?
- Why greet each other in funny or unusual ways?
- How else could we greet each other musically?

BONUS IDEA Consider having the group sing, "We're glad you're here, Kira" (or whatever the child's name is who just sang) in the same musical or comical manner that the young person sang his or her greeting.

Who Do We Appreciate? You! You! You! You!

FOCUS
Kids greet each other with a group cheer.

SPARKS TIE-IN
- Drama/theater
- Sports/athletics

YOU WILL NEED
- A large area

ACTIVITY Have young people sit in a circle with you. Explain that in sports, people cheer on individual athletes, but you don't need to play a sport to be cheered on by our group.

Explain how the greeting will work. The entire group will chant together: "Two. Four. Six. Eight. Who do we appreciate?" Then depending on which young person is featured, the group will say, "Harry! Harry! Harry! Harry!" (or whatever the person's name is) while he or she gets up and runs around the inside of the circle and gives a high five to each group member. Encourage group members to hold their hands up to high-five the young person as they chant his or her name.

Once the young person has run around the entire inside of the circle and sat down again, focus on the person to Harry's right. Repeat the chant and have that child run around the inside of the circle, giving high fives to everyone as the group chants his or her name.

Continue the greeting until everyone in the circle has been featured and run around the inside of the circle.

DISCUSSION QUESTIONS
- Why do sports have cheers and chants?
- What was it like to give everyone a high five as the group was chanting your name?
- Why is it important for us to cheer each other on?
- What other cheer or chant could we adapt to greet each other?

BONUS IDEA If the young people in your group know each other well, have the child running around the inside of the circle pick the next person to be cheered on. Then have that child pick the next person. Continue until everyone has had a turn.

Greeting Toss

FOCUS
Young people greet each other while tossing a ball.

SPARKS TIE-IN
- Dance/movement
- Sports/athletics

YOU WILL NEED
- A soft ball (such as a Nerf ball or an inflatable ball)

ACTIVITY Have young people sit in a circle with you. Give one person a ball.

Explain how the greeting will work. Have the person with the ball choose someone in the circle to roll the ball to. While rolling the ball, he or she says, "Hello, Lori" (or whatever the name is of the child receiving the ball). Lori then gets the ball, rolls it to someone else in the circle, and says, "Hello, Miguel" (or whatever the name is of the child receiving the ball).

Continue the greeting until everyone in the circle has been named and has rolled the ball to someone else.

DISCUSSION QUESTIONS
- What is it like to use some motion and passing a ball to each other during the greeting?
- How easy is it for you to learn other people's names? Why?
- What helps you learn other people's names?
- How else could we use a ball for a greeting?

BONUS IDEA If you're outside or in a gymnasium, consider tossing the ball or bouncing it to each person. Or consider adding a second or third ball to the greeting to have multiple greetings going on simultaneously.

Quick, Quick, Greet!

FOCUS

Young people greet as many people as they can within one minute.

SPARKS TIE-IN

- Dance/movement
- Relationships

YOU WILL NEED

- A clock or timer with a second hand

ACTIVITY Explain how the greeting will work. Each person will mingle around the group and greet as many people as possible within one minute. Have the young people say hello to each other, using their first names. For example, "Hello, Hamad" or "Hello, Bisma."

Start the timer, say "Go," and have the young people do the greeting for one minute.

DISCUSSION QUESTIONS

- What was it like to greet people in a fast way?
- What was it like to hear your name said by different people?
- Why does it matter to know other people's names?
- Why does it matter for other people to know your name?
- How else can we learn each other's names?

BONUS IDEA Consider having young people count how many people they can greet in one minute. Or consider having young people count how many different people they can greet in 20 seconds. Or have young people say their greetings to each other in slow motion.

Frère Jacques Greeting

FOCUS

Kids sing "Frère Jacques" together to greet each other one by one.

SPARKS TIE-IN

- Dance/movement
- Music

YOU WILL NEED

- A large area

ACTIVITY Have everyone sit in a circle with a lot of room between people so that each person can easily jump up when it's his or her turn.

Teach the group these adapted lyrics to "Frère Jacques" while also teaching them the actions that accompany the song:

Group: *Where is (name of child)? Where is (name of child)?*

Child named who jumps up while singing: *Here I am! Here I am!*

Group: *How are you today, hey? How are you today, hey?*

Child named: *I am great. I am great.* (The child then sits down.)

Start the actual song by asking for a volunteer to go first. Sing that child's name first. Then go around the circle counterclockwise for each verse until every child's name has been sung.

DISCUSSION QUESTIONS:

- What was it like to jump up when the group sang your name?
- How was it to sing alone to the group?
- How do greeting activities help us learn each other's names?
- Would you like to do other singing greetings? Why or why not?

BONUS IDEA Once children know the song, they can respond differently according to how they feel. For example, a child might sing, "I am sad" or "I am glad" or "I am scared" or another feeling.

Which Animal Are You?

FOCUS

Young people act out a different animal while greeting each other.

SPARKS TIE-IN

- Animals
- Drama/theater

YOU WILL NEED

- Nothing

ACTIVITY Have everyone sit in a circle. Explain that each person will take turns standing in the middle and silently imitating an animal, such as an elephant, a dog, a monkey, or some other animal. The leader will then choose another child to walk up to the young person in the middle and say: "Hello, (name of child). Which animal are you today?"

The young person imitating the animal will respond: "Hello, (name of child asking the question). I am (name of child acting as the animal), the (name the animal)."

Then, the child who imitated the animal will join the circle. The child who asked what the animal was will imitate a different animal. And the leader will choose another child to approach the child in the middle and repeat the greeting.

Start the activity. Continue until every child has been both in the middle silently imitating an animal and in the middle as the greeting and questioning child.

DISCUSSION QUESTIONS

- What was it like to imitate an animal without making any sound?
- How easy was it to remember the person's name whom you were talking to?
- What do you do if you forget someone's name?
- Why is it important to learn other people's names?
- What else could we imitate for a greeting activity?

BONUS IDEA If you want children to guess the animal that the young person in the middle is imitating, have children go up and greet that person one at a time and say, "Hello (name of child). Are you a (an animal)?" The child who is imitating the animal then responds, "Hello (name of child asking the question)" and either says, "Yes, I am (name of animal)" or "No, I am not (name of animal guessed)." If the child guesses correctly, that child then silently imitates another animal. If the child guesses incorrectly, another child can then go into the middle and guess.

Home Run Greeting

FOCUS
Young people greet each other with baseball actions.

SPARKS TIE-IN
- Dance/movement
- Sports/athletics

YOU WILL NEED
- Nothing

ACTIVITY Have everyone stand in a circle. Explain that each person will take turns saying whether he or she is hitting a single, a double, a triple, or a home run. Then that person will move one person to the right (for a single), two people to the right (for a double), three people to the right (for a triple), or four people to the right (for a home run). After moving to the appropriate place, the child then turns to the person on his or her right and say, "Hello, (name of child). Isn't it a great day to play?"

The child who has been spoken to responds, "Yes it is, (name of child). I am going to hit (a single, a double, a triple, or a home run)." The child then moves to the right the number of spaces that corresponds to a single, a double, a triple, or a home run. That child then greets the young person on his or her right. Continue until every group member has participated.

DISCUSSION QUESTIONS
- What was it like to move around and greet another group member?
- Who figured out in advance whether to choose a single, a double, a triple, or a home run so that you made sure you knew the person's name you would be greeting?

- Why is it important to have fun while learning other people's names?
- What other sport could we adapt into a greeting?

BONUS IDEA Consider adding another dimension to the greeting by giving young people the option to also choose a foul single, a foul double, a foul triple, or a foul home run. If they use the word *foul* in front of the baseball word, they then move that many spaces to the left: one person to the left (for a foul single), two people to the left (for a foul double), three people to the left (for a foul triple), or four people to the left (for a foul home run). The child then greets the young person on his or her left instead of the right.

How Do You Greet People?

FOCUS

Choose specific actions to greet people.

SPARKS TIE-IN

- Relationships
- Living in a specific way

When you're friendly to others, most will act nice to you. In the list below, star the two actions that you currently do to greet other people. Then circle one action to start doing.

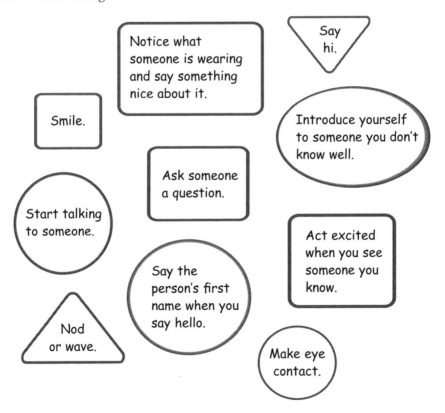

Forward and Backward Greeting

Handout

12

FOCUS
Introduce yourself to others with your first name and the pronunciation of your first name spelled backward.

SPARKS TIE-IN
- Relationships
- Creative arts

On a blank sheet of paper, write your first name in large capital letters, on half of the sheet. For example, if your name is Matt, write MATT.

MATT

Then, write your first name backward in large capital letters, on the opposite side of the paper. For example, if your name is Matt, write TTAM.

TTAM

Now that you've written your name in two ways, fold the paper in half so that the forward name is on one side and the backward name is on the other side. Use the forward name first and introduce yourself to others around you. When your leader says "backward," use your backward name to introduce yourself to others around you.

My Favorite Book Greeting

FOCUS

Identify your favorite book and discover the favorite books of three other people in your group.

SPARKS TIE-IN

- Journalism
- Learning
- Reading

What is your favorite book?
Write its title on the outside of this book.
Write your name on the line below.

My name is _____

Find three other people nearby. Ask them to share the title of their favorite book, then write that title on a blank book image below. Include their name below each book.

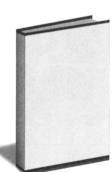

This is _____
favorite book.

This is _____
favorite book.

This is _____
favorite book.

CHAPTER 2

Creating Rules and Routines Activities

The two biggest barriers for a new teacher, coach, or leader are poor group management skills followed by disruptive kids.[1] When kids know what to expect, they're more likely to follow the rules. Yet, too often rules are unspoken, complex, or they don't have the buy-in from the kids. By talking about rules and routines (and creating them with your kids) in the first few days—or weeks—that your group meets, your group members will learn how to behave appropriately so that everyone can make progress and have fun in the process. ▶▶

---

1. David T. Gordon, Rising to the Discipline Challenge, *Harvard Education Letter* (September/October 1999): 1–4.

Positive Rules

FOCUS

Young people reframe negative rules into positive ones.

SPARKS TIE-IN

- Solving social problems
- Living in a specific way

YOU WILL NEED

- 2 large sheets of newsprint or other type of large paper
- Washable markers
- Masking or painter's tape

ACTIVITY With young people, brainstorm a list of rules that they believe would be ideal for your program or classroom. Write what they say on a piece of newsprint. (Or ask for a volunteer to write on the newsprint.) Here are some examples: Stop talking all the time. No fighting. No lying.

Once you have a list, hang it up with tape. Tape the other piece of newsprint to the right of the brainstormed list of rules.

Ask, "What do you notice about these rules?" Give young people time to respond. Ideally, you want someone to say that most of the rules are negative. They're a list of "don'ts" instead of a list of "dos."

Then go through the rules, one at a time, and ask the group to reframe each rule to a positive statement. For example, "Stop talking all the time" could become "Listen more." "No fighting" could become "Be nice to others." "No lying" could become "Tell the truth." Write the new positive rule on the newsprint on the right. If any of the original rules was already said positively, just rewrite it on the new list. Continue until you complete the list.

DISCUSSION QUESTIONS

- What do you think of rules?
- Why does it matter how rules are stated?
- Which rules do you like better: the rules on the left or the ones on the right? Why?
- When are you more likely to follow the rules? Why?
- How else could we create rules?

BONUS IDEA Remove the list on the left that has the negative rules. Keep the list on the right (with the positive rules) posted.

Types of Rules

FOCUS
Young people place rules into major categories.

SPARKS TIE-IN
- Solving social problems
- Learning

YOU WILL NEED
- 2 large sheets of newsprint or other type of large paper
- Washable markers
- Masking or painter's tape

ACTIVITY If your group already has a list of rules, use your list. Otherwise, brainstorm a list of rules with young people, rules they believe would be ideal for your program or classroom. Write what they say on a newsprint. (Or ask for a volunteer to write on the newsprint.) Here are some examples: Respect each other. Take care of the playground equipment. Don't interrupt others.

Once you have a list, hang it up with tape. Tape the other piece of newsprint to the right of the brainstormed list of rules. On the second piece of newsprint create two columns: "Rules on how to treat yourself and others" (left-hand column) and "Rules on how to treat property," such as your own things and the group's things (right-hand column).

Say, "Most rules fit into these two broad categories: rules for how to treat yourself and others, and rules for how to treat property and things. Let's go through our list of rules and figure out which rules fit into which category."

Discuss the rules, one at a time. As a group, decide which category each rule fits into. For example, "Respect each other" would fit into the left-hand column about how to treat yourself and others. "Take care of the playground equipment" would fit into the right-hand column about how to treat property. "Don't interrupt others" would fit into the left-hand column. Continue until you have placed all of the rules into the two categories. If you have rules that don't seem to fit either category, discuss whether you could add a third category for those rules and what that category would be called.

Once you finish, talk about which column is the longest and which is the shortest. Young people usually can think of a lot of rules about themselves and others. Encourage them to brainstorm other rules for the shorter category. Then review all of your lists.

DISCUSSION QUESTIONS

- How is it helpful to place rules into categories?
- How can categories help us to simplify rules so they don't seem so overwhelming?
- Which category is most important? Why?
- How can placing rules into categories make it easier to follow the rules?
- How else can we think about rules?

BONUS IDEA Examine rules in each category. Work to combine rules within categories to have fewer rules.

The Purpose of Rules

FOCUS
Young people discuss the purpose of rules.

SPARKS TIE-IN
- Living in a specific way
- Solving social problems

YOU WILL NEED
- 1 piece of 8½" x 11" white paper for each small group
- 1 pencil for each small group
- 1 large sheet of newsprint or other type of large paper
- Washable markers
- Masking or painter's tape

ACTIVITY Hang up the newsprint in front of the group. Create small groups of three to four young people. Give each group a piece of paper and one pencil. Ask for each group to designate a volunteer to write the group's ideas on the paper.

Explain that you want small groups to brainstorm a list of why rules are important. Give young people two to three minutes to do this.

When they finish, ask for a volunteer to write what the small groups report on the large piece of newsprint hanging in front of the group. Then ask individual groups to tell only one reason why rules are important. (If you allow one group to report all of their ideas, some groups may not have anything new to add.) Continue going from group to group until all of the ideas have been added to the large newsprint.

End with a large-group discussion about the importance of rules.

DISCUSSION QUESTIONS

- Why do rules matter?
- When is it easy for you to follow rules? When is it hard?
- What would happen if we didn't have any rules?
- Why talk about why rules matter? Why not just make rules and expect people to follow them?
- How else can we discuss the purpose of rules?

BONUS IDEA Discuss why it matters who makes the rules. Is it easier to follow rules that you help create or rules that others make for you? Why?

My Dream

FOCUS

Young people name their biggest dream for being in your group.

SPARKS TIE-IN

- Photography/film
- Writing

YOU WILL NEED

- A camera (digital, Polaroid, or film)
- Any camera supplies (such as the cord, batteries, and memory card for a digital camera or film for a film or Polaroid® camera)
- 1 piece of 8½" x 11" white paper for each young person
- 1 pencil for each young person
- A place to display the photos and dreams, such as a bulletin board, a wall, a door, or a handmade booklet you create with each young person

ACTIVITY Give each young person a piece of paper and a pencil. Ask the group members to think about one goal (or dream) they have for participating in your group. For example, if you have a classroom, a dream could be to learn to write in cursive better. If you have a soccer team, a dream could be to listen more to the coach. If you have a club, a dream could be to help others in the club.

Encourage young people to write their dreams in just one sentence, starting with their first name. Have them use their best printing or cursive since their dreams will be on display. For example, Omar hopes to listen more to the coach. Gabby dreams of writing in cursive better.

As young people finish, have them bring their dream to you. Take a photo of the child. When everyone has finished, you should have collected each child's written dream and taken a photo of each one.

Create a display on the wall, bulletin board, or in a booklet that you distribute. Place the photo of each young person with his or her dream. Give kids time to look at the display and compare dreams. (This also helps them get to connect names with faces.)

DISCUSSION QUESTIONS

- How easy was it for you to choose a dream or goal?
- Why is it important to have a dream or a goal?
- Is your dream or goal similar to someone else's? If so, whose?
- How do you make your dream or goal come true?
- How else can we talk about our dreams?

BONUS IDEA Halfway through your season, quarter, or year, bring out the display of dreams and photos. Revisit them with the young people in the group. Ask how they're progressing toward their dream. Help them make concrete steps if they're having trouble making progress. Then revisit each child's dream at the end of your season, quarter, or year to mark how much progress they made (even if it was just a little).

Why People Break Rules

FOCUS
Young people identify different reasons why people break rules.

SPARKS TIE-IN
- Solving social problems
- Speech

YOU WILL NEED
- 1 large sheet of newsprint or other type of large paper
- Washable markers
- Masking or painter's tape

ACTIVITY Hang up the sheet of newsprint. As a group, brainstorm a list of 9 or 10 rules for your group that are tempting to break.

Have each young person find a partner. If you have an odd number of group members, make one group of three.

Explain that you want each group to pick one rule from the list on the newsprint. The group will then think of two or three reasons why young people might break that rule. Each group needs to come up with a reason for each member of the group. If the group has two people, the group thinks of two reasons. If the group has three people, they need to come up with three reasons.

If groups are having trouble thinking of ideas, you could get them started by providing some examples, such as these: You're late so you were in a hurry (this works for the rules of not running in the hallway or missing a warm-up). You didn't know the rule existed. You didn't think you would get caught. You've seen other people break the rule. You didn't think the rule was important. You got caught up in an activity and didn't realize you were breaking the rule.

Give groups time to do the activity. When they finish, have the small groups take turns standing in front of the entire group and ask each person in the group to name a reason why that rule could be broken. Continue until every group (and every young person has spoken).

DISCUSSION QUESTIONS
- How easy was it to name reasons why people break rules? Why?
- Do you think most people break rules on purpose or by mistake? Why?
- Are people more likely to break rules when the rules aren't enforced? Why or why not?
- Do you find it easier to follow the rules or break them? Why?
- Why does it matter to follow the rules?
- How else can we make rules that aren't easy to break?

BONUS IDEA Have the group analyze a rule for adults that gets broken often, such as driving over the speed limit. Discuss why they think adults break rules. Do adults break rules for the same reasons as young people? Why or why not?

Punishments versus Logical Consequences

FOCUS

Young people identify the differences between punishments and logical consequences.

SPARKS TIE-IN

- Learning
- Solving social problems

YOU WILL NEED

- 1 large sheet of newsprint or other type of large paper
- Washable markers
- Masking or painter's tape

ACTIVITY Hang up the sheet of newsprint. Create three columns with these headings: Broken Rule, Punishment, and Natural or Logical Consequence.

Say: "When people break rules, they're often punished. Punishments are given in anger. They're about stopping or controlling the behavior, and they often are arbitrary, which means they don't always fit with the broken rule. What are some examples of punishments?"

Give young people time to respond. Examples could include getting grounded for life, being hit for misbehaving, being threatened for breaking a rule, or getting yelled at.

Say: "Natural or logical consequences are about responding to a broken rule with empathy. It's about teaching the young person what he or she did wrong and giving the rule breaker a choice. What are examples of logical or natural consequences?"

Give young people time to respond. They may have a harder time thinking of these type of consequences since punishments are often more pervasive in our society. Here are some examples: You didn't finish your homework, so you failed the assignment. You didn't hang up your coat, so it got dirty by everybody stepping on it.

Ask the group to name a rule that gets broken often. Write it on the left-hand, "Broken Rule," column of the newsprint. For example, the designated person forgets to bring snacks to practice. Then ask: "What would be a punishment for breaking this rule?" Encourage the group to brainstorm ideas. Then have the group vote for the most extreme punishment. For example, the person isn't allowed to practice that day or the person is yelled at. Write what the group decided in the middle, "Punishment," column.

Then ask: "What would be a natural or logical consequence for breaking this rule?" Encourage the group to brainstorm ideas. Then have the group vote for the best natural or logical consequence. For example, everyone gets hungry because there isn't any snack. So since everyone went hungry, the designated person was more likely to remember to bring snacks.

Draw a line under the example. Do a second or a third broken rule so that the group practices and learns the difference between punishments and natural and logical consequences.

DISCUSSION QUESTIONS

- What's easier to think of: punishments or consequences? Why?
- Why are punishments more memorable than consequences?
- When you're being punished, what do you tend to think? Why?
- Which is more respectful: punishments or consequences? Why?
- Why is it important to have consequences for broken rules?
- How else can we think of consequences?

BONUS IDEA Focus on a rule that often gets broken in your group. Brainstorm solutions of how to respond to this situation where young people can learn how to follow the rule without punishment.

The Quiet Signal

FOCUS

Young people choose an indoor and an outdoor quiet signal that gets their attention.

SPARKS TIE-IN

- Comedy
- Drama/theater

YOU WILL NEED

- A whistle
- A humorous sound maker (such as a screech, a party noisemaker, burping, or an unusual sound from a computer)
- A large area

ACTIVITY Explain that there are times when the group gets noisy and that everyone needs to quiet down and listen. This can happen both when the group is inside and when the group is outside.

Say: "We're going to try some different indoor signals to see which one works best for the group. Everyone spread out. Go ahead and talk. I'm going to raise my hand at some point, which means to stop talking and quiet down. As soon as you see my hand go up, quiet down and raise your hand as well. Let's see how quickly the entire group can quiet down."

Give the young people time to mingle and talk. At some point, raise your hand. See how long it takes for the group to quiet down.

Then try another signal, such as raising both arms above your head. See how long it takes for the group to quiet down. Then try another signal, such as clapping your hands. Then try the humorous signal, such as screeching or using a party noisemaker.

After you've tried four different signals, have the group vote on which signal works best. Use that one from then on. (But be open to using the other options if kids stop responding to the one signal.)

If your group sometimes goes outdoors, work through this activity outside as well. Try a whistle. Then try waving both arms. Then try yelling "come in" two times and then try having the young people yell "come in" two times as they hear it. (That way no one loses his or her voice.) Again, vote on an outside signal for the group to follow.

DISCUSSION QUESTIONS

- When is it hard to notice a signal to quiet down?
- Why are some signals easier to notice than others?
- Why does the quiet-down signal need to be different when we're inside versus when we're outside?
- Why does a group need a quiet-down signal?
- What other signals could we consider?

BONUS IDEA Assign a different young person to give the signal during a group time. This gives young people the chance to lead the group, and it also encourages them to respect each group member—not just the adult leader.

Places for Rules

FOCUS

Young people identify different places and settings for having rules.

SPARKS TIE-IN

- Advocacy
- Nature, ecology, environment
- Solving social problems

YOU WILL NEED

- 1 large sheet of newsprint or other type of large paper
- Washable markers
- Masking or painter's tape

ACTIVITY Hang up the newsprint in front of the group. Create small groups of three or four young people.

Explain how your group tends to spend most of its group time in one place. (It may be a classroom, the room where your club meets, or on a practice field.) Give the small groups time to think of other places where it's also important to follow rules. After about three to four minutes, have the small groups take turns naming places where rules are important; limit each group to naming one place per turn. Write their ideas on the newsprint. Examples include bus, lunchroom, bathroom, playground, gym, or outside area waiting for parents or guardians to arrive.

Ask: "Which rules are the same for all these locations?" Give young people time to answer. Then ask: "Which rules are different for each location?" Discuss.

End by saying: "We have rules wherever we are. Sometimes we may think that some areas don't have rules. Yet they do. It's important to know and follow the rules—no matter where we are."

DISCUSSION QUESTIONS
- Who enforces the rules in each place we mentioned?
- Why is it easier to follow the rules in some places than others?
- Why can it seem that there aren't any rules before our group starts and after we're finished?
- How can we be more mindful of the rules no matter where we are?

BONUS IDEA Discuss how the time of day also affects how easy or difficult it is to follow the rules. Talk about which times are easiest and which are hardest and why.

Worthwhile Rules

FOCUS
Young people vote on which attributes of rules are most important.

SPARKS TIE-IN
- Living in a specific way
- Solving social problems

YOU WILL NEED
- 1 large sheet of newsprint or other type of large paper
- 1 washable marker for each young person plus 1 black marker for you
- Masking or painter's tape

ACTIVITY Hang up the newsprint in front of the group. Write these words and phrases (with an line under each phrase and room for young people to write): leader makes rules, everyone makes rules together, creates safety, creates a strong team, solves problems, blames the rule breaker, creates anger, and creates peace.

Explain that worthwhile rules have certain things in common. Create small groups of three or four young people and then ask them to talk about the options listed on the newsprint. As groups discuss, have members of one group bring their markers to the newsprint. Have each young person vote for the most important items on the newsprint by adding a tally mark under the phrase. (For ease in tallying up the votes later, encourage young people to group the slashes in fives. The fifth tally mark should be made diagonally through the other four marks in a grouping.)

Once everyone in one group finishes, have another group go up to vote. Continue until everyone has voted. Then add up the votes and circle the winning phrases in another color (such as red or blue).

DISCUSSION QUESTIONS

- What did you think of this activity?
- Why did you vote for some words and phrases and not others?
- Why does it matter how rules are created? (Compare the votes for the phrases "leader makes rules" versus "everyone makes rules together.")
- Why does it matter what the rules create? (Compare the votes for the phrases for "creates safety," "creates a strong team," "creates anger," and "creates peace.")
- Which place has the best rules? Why? How do you know?
- How else can we create worthwhile rules?

BONUS IDEA Repeat the activity and add other words and phrases. Have young people vote for "Worthless Rules." This often generates a lively discussion, especially when you compare worthwhile rules to worthless ones.

Many Rules versus Few Rules

FOCUS

Identify your thoughts and feelings about different lists of rules.

SPARKS TIE-IN

- Reading
- Solving social problems

Rule List 1

1. Take care of yourself.
2. Take care of others around you.
3. Take care of your things and the things around you.

Rule List 2

1. No yelling.
2. No pushing.
3. Shut the door behind you every time you open the door.
4. Take turns with others.
5. Put things away after using them.
6. Wash your hands before you go home.
7. Don't bring snacks with you.
8. Listen to the leader.
9. Participate fully.
10. Don't interrupt others.

What two feelings do you get from Rule List 1?

1. _____
   _____

2. _____
   _____

What two feelings do you get from Rule List 2?

1. _____
   _____

2. _____
   _____

Which rule list do you like better? Why?

Rules Here and at Home

Handout

FOCUS

Encourage your family to have similar rules at home as the ones in our group.

SPARKS TIE-IN

- Family
- Solving social problems

Dear Families,

Our group has been talking a lot about how to make our group work well.

That involves our expectations, our goals, and our rules. It's easier to follow rules during our group when families talk about the importance of these rules at home.

It's even more effective if you have rules at home that are similar to the ones on our list. We hope you post this list at home and talk about these rules with your kids.

Thank you!

List your group rules here:

_____

Sign your name here.

Role Models and Rules

FOCUS
Examine how your role model deals with rules.

SPARKS TIE-IN
- Leadership
- Relationships

 Who is your role model?

 Who else is your role model?

 Which rules does your role model follow?

 Which rules does this role model follow?

 What do you learn from your role model?

 What do you learn from this role model?

CHAPTER 3

Sharing Activities

While helping kids to learn each other's names is important, you want kids to also go deeper with the relationships that they have with you, the other adults in your group, and the other young people. Relationships are built when people share information about themselves, when they talk together, and when they take time to really get to know each other. These activities encourage young people to reveal more about themselves and their interests. ▶▶

Snowball Pile

FOCUS

Young people get to know other people with this unusual mixer.

SPARKS TIE-IN

- Learning
- Relationships

YOU WILL NEED

- 1 piece of white paper for each young person
- 1 pen or pencil for each young person
- A large area

ACTIVITY Give each young person a piece of paper and a pen or pencil. Have each young person write his or her first and last name on the piece of paper and then wad up the paper like a snowball.

After everyone has finished, have young people create a circle. Ask everyone to toss his or her snowball paper into the middle of the circle.

Ask for a volunteer. Have that person go the snowball pile and choose one snowball paper. That person then opens up the snowball and reads aloud the name written on the paper. The person named then raises his or her hand so that the person in the middle knows who that person is.

The person in the middle then walks over to that person and says, "Hi _____ (saying the name of the person) I'm _____ (saying his or her name)." The person with the snowball then asks the person whom he or she has just greeted one question. For example, "How many people are in your family?" "What's your favorite thing to do when you're not in school?" or "What's your favorite food?"

The person then answers the question and says, "Thanks _____ (saying the name of the person who asked the question)."

The person who asked the question keeps holding on to the snowball paper and joins the circle. The person who just answered the question then walks to the middle of the circle, picks up a snowball, and repeats the activity.

Continue until all the paper snowballs have been chosen.

DISCUSSION QUESTIONS

- What interesting fact did you learn about someone in our group from the questions asked?
- Which did you like better: asking the question or answering the question? Why?
- Why is it important to get to know other people in our group?
- How else could we use snowballs to get to know others in our group?

BONUS IDEA Collect all the snowballs after your activity. When kids get restless and aren't paying attention, have a quick snowball fight. End the activity by having each young person grab one nearby snowball. Then have kids open up their snowball, find the person named on the snowball, and sit with that person when you return to your usual activity.

Mystery Person

FOCUS

Young people identify three facts about themselves while others guess who the mystery person is.

SPARKS TIE-IN

- Learning
- Relationships

YOU WILL NEED

- 1 piece of white paper for each young person
- 1 pen or pencil for each young person

ACTIVITY Give each young person a piece of paper and a pen or pencil. Tell them that they will not write their names on their papers. Have each person write the numbers one through three on their paper, and then ask them to write three facts about themselves that most people in your group may not know. For example: 1. I'm the middle child of three kids. 2. My family has visited

Colombia. 3. My favorite book is *Harry Potter and the Half-Blood Prince.*
Make sure young people don't see what other group members write.

Have young people fold their papers in half when they finish. Then collect all the papers. (Consider adding your own into the mix.)

Ask for a volunteer. Have that person stand in front of the group, choose a paper, and read aloud the list of three things from one of the papers. Then ask the volunteer to guess who might have written that list. After three incorrect guesses, have the person who wrote the paper jump up and say, "That's me!"

The person who identified himself or herself then goes to the front of the group, chooses a paper, and reads aloud what's on the paper. That person then guesses, and you do the activity again.

Continue until all the papers have been read aloud.

DISCUSSION QUESTIONS

- What was the most interesting fact you learned about someone in our group?
- Which did you like better: writing three facts about yourself or guessing which facts were written by which person? Why?
- Which would be more difficult: figuring out the mystery person in a group of strangers or in a group of your best friends? Why?
- Why is it important to learn unusual things about people in our group?
- How else can we get to know each other?

BONUS IDEA Use this activity to help group members learn more about the adult leaders in your group, volunteers, or important people in your field or activity. For example, if your group is a soccer team, you can find three facts about Cristiano Ronaldo of Spain or Mia Hamm of the United States.

Taking Sides

FOCUS

Young people learn more about themselves and each other by taking sides.

SPARKS TIE-IN

- Advocacy
- Learning
- Relationships

YOU WILL NEED

- A large area with two distinct sides

ACTIVITY Explain that you're going to do an activity where young people will take a stand for who they are while getting to know others in the group better.

Have everyone stand up. Explain that you're going to give the group two options. Those who choose the first option will run to the left side of your area. Those who choose the second option will run to the right side of your area. (It helps to point to each side as you read the options to make it easier for kids to know where to move.)

Say: "Those who are vegetarian, move to the left. Those who eat meat, move to the right." Give young people time to move. Then have young people look around to see who is on which side of the room or outside area.

Then explain that you'll say two more options. The first options will run to the left (or stay on the left-hand side if that's where they already are), and the second choice will run to the right. Read aloud one of the statements below:

- You like waking up early or you like sleeping in.
- You've lived in the same home your entire life or you've moved around.
- Spring is your favorite season or autumn is your favorite season.
- You like dogs or you like cats.
- You were born in this state or province, or you were born somewhere else.
- You speak one language or you speak more than one language.
- You like being with lots of friends or you prefer to be with one best friend.

Then read other statements aloud until you've done them all. If you wish, you can end with a statement where everyone moves to one side, such as, "If you're in _____ (your name)'s group, run to the right."

DISCUSSION QUESTIONS

- Which statement was hard for you to pick a side? Why?
- Which statement did you notice the most people agreed with you?
- Which statement did you notice that most people did not agree with you and were on the other side of the room?
- Why is it important to get to know others in our group?
- How else can we learn more about each other?

BONUS IDEA Encourage young people to get to know each other more by pausing after each statement and debriefing it. For example, for the statement about languages, ask each person on the "more than one language side" to identify which languages they speak.

Where in the World?

29

FOCUS

Young people investigate where they'd like to travel.

SPARKS TIE-IN

- Computer
- Learning
- Journalism
- Speech

YOU WILL NEED

- A computer with Internet access for each young person (or each pair of young people)
- 1 piece of 8½" x 11" white paper for each young person
- 1 pencil for each young person

ACTIVITY Find a bank of computers to use at a school media center, public library, or local organization.

Explain that individuals are going to explore where they'd like to travel in the world. Depending on how many computers you have, have young people either work alone, in pairs, or in small groups. If small groups are working together, make sure each young person has time to research a place he or she would like to visit.

Give each young person a piece of paper and a pencil. Then give them time to identify another country they would like to visit and find three interesting facts about that country. Have them write their name, the country they chose, and the three facts on the piece of paper. Encourage young people to use these websites to gather information:

- Info Please (www.infoplease.com/countries.html)
- Fact Monster (www.factmonster.com/countries.html)
- Central Intelligence Agency, the World Factbook (www.cia.gov/library/publications/the-world-factbook)

After young people finish, ask for volunteers to share what they discovered and wrote.

DISCUSSION QUESTIONS

- What did you think of researching a country through these websites?
- Which website did you like the best? Why?
- Why does it matter to learn about other places in the world?
- How else can we learn about other countries?

BONUS IDEA Ask group members to identify the countries they have visited. Make a group list. Then have group members talk a bit about the countries they have visited.

My Favorite

FOCUS

Young people tell about their favorite things.

SPARKS TIE-IN

- Learning
- Relationships
- Speech

YOU WILL NEED

- Nothing

ACTIVITY Explain that you're going to do a sharing activity where young people will name their favorite thing in the topic you name.

Create small groups of three or four young people. Then name the first topic: your favorite food. Give young people time to discuss their favorite foods in their small groups. Then have the small groups take turns standing in front of the entire group with each person in the small group naming his or her favorite food.

Once all the groups have shared. Give them another topic. Consider these topics:

- favorite color
- favorite book
- favorite place to go on vacation
- favorite movie
- favorite item you own
- favorite game to play
- favorite sport
- favorite music

Repeat the activity as often as you wish with a different topic.

DISCUSSION QUESTIONS

- Was it easier or harder to stand up in front of the entire group when you had your small group standing with you instead of standing alone?

- How often did you discover that someone else in our group had the same favorite thing as you do?
- Why is it important to tell your favorite things to others?
- How does knowing more about group members help our group time?
- What other favorites can we find out about each other?

BONUS IDEA Consider changing the activity to the "Best of." Have young people talk about the "best" experience they had eating with their family, going on a trip, spending time with a friend, having fun at school, and so on.

In One Breath

FOCUS
Young people tell as much as they can about themselves in one exhalation.

SPARKS TIE-IN
- Comedy
- Learning
- Relationships
- Speech

YOU WILL NEED
- Nothing

ACTIVITY Have young people sit in a circle. Ask for a volunteer. Have that person stand up.

Explain that the volunteer will start the activity. He or she will take a deep breath in and then say as many facts as possible about himself or herself in one long exhale. As soon as the volunteer runs out of breath, he or she needs to stop. The person on the volunteer's right will count how many facts are said during the exhale.

If young people aren't sure what to talk about, suggest that they name all their favorite things, activities, areas of the country they've visited, favorite school subjects, family member names, or any fact about themselves.

Do the activity. After the volunteer has run out of breath, have the person on the right say how many facts the speaker stated. Then ask the group if they have any questions for the volunteer. After three questions, ask for another volunteer to do the activity.

Repeat the activity a number of times. See who can say the most facts in one breath.

DISCUSSION QUESTIONS

- How hard was it to name a lot of facts in one breath?
- What made this activity interesting compared to other activities that we do?
- What new fact did you learn about someone in our group?
- Why is it important to get to know others in our group?
- How else can we get to know each other?

BONUS IDEA Add more comedy to this activity by bringing a bunch of helium balloons and then helping the volunteer take one inhalation of the helium from one balloon before talking.

Star of the Day

32

FOCUS

Young people take turns being the star of the day for your group.

SPARKS TIE-IN

- Learning
- Relationships
- Speech

YOU WILL NEED

- 1 piece of paper for each young person
- A pen or pencil, or a computer and printer
- A photocopy of your group roster

ACTIVITY Designate a different day for each person in your group to be "the star of the day." For your first "star," choose someone who speaks easily in front of your group. Send a note home with that person explaining that the person will be the star of the day for your group and the date that will happen. In the note, encourage the young person to bring three special items on that day to share with the group.

On the day that the person is the star, take time to have that person stand in front of your group, show the three items he or she brought, and explain why those items are important to him or her. Encourage group members to ask questions to get to know the star more. (If a star forgets to bring items, have the star talk about three things he or she would have brought.)

Then give written instructions to the next person who will be the star of the day. Explain that each group member will get a turn to be the star.

DISCUSSION QUESTIONS

- What did you learn about our star of the day?
- How did it feel to be the star of the day?
- Why is it important to be a star from time to time?
- How else can we recognize each other?

BONUS IDEA Consider buying or making a crown for the star to wear during the group time. Or make some type of special name tag to signify that the child was a star. This allows young people to take a memento home, and each child will get one over the course of your season, quarter, or club meeting time.

Me, Too!

FOCUS

Young people discover what they have in common with other group members.

SPARKS TIE-IN

- Learning
- Relationships
- Speech

YOU WILL NEED

- Nothing

ACTIVITY Ask for a volunteer to start the activity. Have that person stand in front of your group. (Have the rest of the group sit.)

Ask the volunteer: "What's your favorite activity to do after school?"

After the volunteer has answered, ask if anyone in the group would answer the question in the same way. If so, those people should stand up and say, "Me too!"

Give young people time to notice who is standing and that they have that favorite activity in common.

Then have everyone sit down. Ask for another volunteer. Have that person stand in front of the group. Ask the volunteer: "What's your favorite activity to do on a weekend?"

After the volunteer has answered, ask if anyone in the group would answer the question in the same way. If so, those people should stand up and say, "Me too!" Give young people time to notice who is standing and that they have that activity in common.

Continue the activity with different volunteers. Consider asking one of these questions each time:

- What's your favorite activity to do when you're sick?
- What's your favorite activity to do in the winter?
- What's your favorite activity to do in the summer?
- What's your favorite activity to do inside?
- What's your favorite activity to do outside?

- What's your favorite activity to do on Thanksgiving?
- What's your favorite activity to do at school?

DISCUSSION QUESTIONS

- How often did you find you had an activity in common with someone else?
- How does it feel to have something in common with someone in our group?
- Why does it matter to have things in common with group members?
- How else can we learn more about each other?

BONUS IDEA See if any of your group members would like to think up additional questions and ask them. Often young people come up with insightful questions, and leading the group in this way empowers them.

My Family

FOCUS
Young people talk about their families.

SPARKS TIE-IN
- Family
- Learning
- Relationships

YOU WILL NEED
- A large space

ACTIVITY Have young people spread out and sit. Explain that you're going to do an activity where young people will stand if you name something about their family that's true.

Say: "You have four living grandparents." Encourage young people to stand if that's true. Have them look around to see how many kids are sitting and standing. Then ask them all to sit again.

Say something else about families. Consider these statements:

- You have at least one brother.
- You have at least one sister.
- You are an only child.
- You're the oldest of the kids in your family.
- You're the youngest of the kids in your family.
- You live with a single parent.
- You live with two parents.
- You have been to a family reunion.
- You have family members who speak more than one language.

Say a number of statements so that young people can learn about each other's families.

DISCUSSION QUESTIONS
- What did you discover about other group members' families?
- How many group members have family characteristics like yours?
- Why does it matter to talk about our families?
- How can we learn more about each other?

BONUS IDEA If you discover something unique about your group members (such as a lot of them are immigrants or many of them speak other languages), celebrate that fact. If you have many immigrants, count up how many countries are represented in your group.

Speedy Share

FOCUS
Young people tell about themselves in a speedy circle share.

SPARKS TIE-IN
- Comedy
- Learning
- Relationships

YOU WILL NEED
- Nothing

ACTIVITY Have young people sit or stand in a circle. (If you have more than 20 group members present, consider creating smaller groups of no more than 20 young people.)

Explain that your group is going to do a "speedy share." Ask for a volunteer. Explain that you'll ask a question, and the volunteer will quickly answer it. Then, moving clockwise around the circle, the next person will answer the question as quickly as possible. Encourage young people to talk fast.

Begin by asking, "What makes a good friend?" Then see how quickly the answers fly around the circle. When you get back to the volunteer, ask another question. Consider these questions:

- What do you like best about your family?
- What's your favorite pet?
- If you could go anywhere in the world, where would you go?
- What do you eat too much of that you shouldn't?
- What healthy food should you eat more of?
- What word would you use to describe yourself?
- What makes you laugh?

Ask a number of questions, encouraging the group to answer faster and faster each time.

DISCUSSION QUESTIONS
- What did you think of this activity?

- Would you have liked to have sat in a different part of the circle? If so, which part? Why?
- Did you learn anything about anybody else, or was this just too fast?
- Why is it important to do different activities as a group?
- How else can we have fun and learn more about each other at the same time?

BONUS IDEA Add more challenge to the activity. Instead of starting with the same volunteer, explain that you'll pick a different volunteer to start each time. That way young people need to be ready at all times.

You and Me: What's in Common?

FOCUS

Find three things you have in common with someone else.

SPARKS TIE-IN

- Relationships
- Computers
- Writing

Find a partner. Together, read through each category below and name your favorite. How does it compare to your partner's favorite? Identify three things you have common.

- favorite meal
- favorite book
- favorite sport
- favorite video game
- favorite music group
- favorite season of the year

- favorite drink
- favorite store
- favorite website
- favorite snack
- favorite TV show
- favorite animal to have as a pet

Write three things you have in common with your partner:

1.

2.

3.

How Are We Feeling Today?

Handout

37

FOCUS
Discover how 10 group members are feeling on this day.

SPARKS TIE-IN
- Journalism
- Learning
- Relationships

Begin by marking a tally under the feeling that best describes how you are feeling today. When you finish, find 10 other people in our group to mark what their feelings are today. Then add up the numbers and see which feeling is most common.

Excited

Sad

Scared

Happy

Angry

Shy

Ask yourself these questions:

- How do your numbers compare to what others in your group found?

- Why does it matter how we feel?

About You: From A to Z

FOCUS

Name facts about you using each letter of the alphabet.

SPARKS TIE-IN

- Learning
- Living in a specific way
- Writing

Using each letter of the alphabet, write one fact about yourself. For example, if you like apples, books, and you think of yourself as caring, write "apples" next to A, "books" next to B, and "caring" next to C.

A   N

B   O

C   P

D   Q

E   R

F   S

G   T

H   U

I   V

J   W

K   X

L   Y

M   Z

Ask yourself these questions:

- Which letter would you repeat to replace letters that were harder to complete?

- What did you discover about yourself?

CHAPTER 4

Community-Building Activities

A strong group, team, or class has a cohesive sense of community. Community-building activities do just that: They teach kids to work together in fun ways so that they build relationships as a group. This involves breaking up cliques and small groups so that kids get to know each other more and learn to trust others. The activities in this chapter build a sense of community in nonthreatening ways, helping kids to open up and work together. ▶▶

Chase or Chased

FOCUS

Youth build community by playing this creative version of tag.

SPARKS TIE-IN

- Dance/movement
- Sports/athletics
- Outdoor life (if you do this outside)

YOU WILL NEED

- A large area

ACTIVITY Have young people spread out in a large area, either inside or outside. Explain that you're going to name a category. Anyone who fits that category will chase other young people who don't fit that category in a game of tag. If you are being chased and get tagged, you need to sit down.

Name a category where young people can clearly see who fits (and doesn't fit the category). For example: Anyone wearing eyeglasses.

The kids wearing eyeglasses then chase the young people who aren't wearing eyeglasses. Keep playing until everyone without eyeglasses is tagged and sitting down.

Then play again with a different category. Consider these categories:

- has long hair
- wears blue jeans
- wears braces (if you have a lot of young people with braces)
- wears tennis shoes

Choose categories that kids have a lot of control over, such as clothes they're wearing or hairstyles since young people may feel singled out by race or ethnicity if you choose something they're born with, such as skin color.

Play a few more times with different categories.

DISCUSSION QUESTIONS

- Which did you like more: chasing others or being chased? Why?
- How did this game help you to notice other people more?
- Why is it important to have fun with the people we spend time with?
- What other categories should we add next time we play?

BONUS IDEA Do the activity with two volunteers being "it." Encourage these two to strategize how to tag the most people before they begin.

Creative Lineup

FOCUS

Young people line up according to shoe size without speaking.

SPARKS TIE-IN
- Dance/movement
- Leadership
- Sports/athletics

YOU WILL NEED
- A large area

ACTIVITY Have young people spread out. Explain that you're going to do a silent community-building activity. Say that you want group members to line up according to shoe size—without speaking—with one end of the line being the smallest shoe size and the other end being the largest shoe size. Remind the group that no one can speak.

Give young people time to do the activity. Applaud their efforts when they finish.

DISCUSSION QUESTIONS
- What was most difficult about this activity?
- How did you communicate with each other without speaking?
- Who became the leaders during this activity? Why?
- Why is it important to build community among group members?
- How else can we work together?

BONUS IDEA Do the activity again according to height. Or see if group members can figure out how to complete the activity by birth date without speaking.

Pipeline

FOCUS

Youth build community by creating a pipeline.

SPARKS TIE-IN

- Engineering
- Leadership
- Learning

YOU WILL NEED

- 1 empty toilet paper roll for each young person
- A couple of marbles

ACTIVITY Give each young person an empty toilet paper roll. Have them form a line with a clear beginning and ending.

Explain that the group is going to move a marble from person to person through the empty toilet paper rolls without touching it. If the marble falls or someone touches the marble, then the group needs to start over.

Start the activity. At first, it may seem impossible, but group members can figure out ways to work together to send the marble down the line.

DISCUSSION QUESTIONS

- At what point did you think this activity was impossible? Why?
- What was the biggest obstacle to overcome in this activity?
- How did group members work together to send the marble down the line?
- Why is it important to work together as a group?
- How else can we build community?

BONUS IDEA Once group members become adept at sending one marble down the line, have multiple marbles going simultaneously. Once a marble reaches the third person, start another marble down the line. See how many marbles the group can send down the line within a certain amount of time.

Group Applause

FOCUS
Young people learn each other's names as a way to build community.

SPARKS TIE-IN
- Dance/movement
- Learning

YOU WILL NEED
- Nothing

ACTIVITY Have young people stand in a circle. Say your first name. Clap your hands once for each syllable for your first name as you say it. For example, if your first name is Shoshanna, you would clap three times for your three-syllable name. Then ask the group to repeat your name and clap three times.

Explain that you're going to do this activity by going around the circle. Have the person on your right go next. That person says his or her name, such as Michael, and claps once for each syllable. For the name Michael, this would mean two claps. Then have the group repeat that person's name while clapping the correct number of syllables.

Continue around the circle until everyone has given his or her name this way.

Then repeat. Start with another person in the circle. Move to the left around the circle, saying and clapping the names faster this time.

DISCUSSION QUESTIONS
- How did this activity help you remember other group members' names?
- Which version of the game did you like most: the first time we played it or the second time? Why?
- Why is it important to build community in our group?
- How else could we do this activity to make it even more fun?

BONUS IDEA Repeat the activity by last name.

Lily Pad Hop

FOCUS

Young people build community by playing this game together.

SPARKS TIE-IN
- Dance/movement
- Music
- Sports/athletics

YOU WILL NEED
- A large area
- Music with speakers
- About 20 pieces of 8½" x 11" green paper

ACTIVITY Spread out the pieces of green paper in a playing area. (If you have fewer than 20 young people present, put out only the same number of green papers as you have young people.)

Explain that you're going to play an active game. Young people will skip around the area while the music plays. As soon as the music stops, they need to find a green piece of paper (the "lily pads") and touch it. More than one person can touch the same lily pad.

Have young people spread out. Start the music. Have them hop around the area. At some point, stop the music while kids rush to touch a lily pad.

Start the music again. Remove one of the lily pads from the playing area. At some point, stop the music and see where kids end up.

Continue repeating the activity, removing one lily pad each time. See how young people work together as more and more of them need to touch fewer lily pads at the same time.

DISCUSSION QUESTIONS
- How did the way you touch a lily pad change from the beginning of the game to the ending of it? Why?
- How did you figure out ways to get a lot of people touching only a few lily pads?
- Would you like this activity more or less if we eliminated group members from the game who couldn't find a way to touch a lily pad? Why?

- Why does it matter to build community in our group?
- How else can we learn to work together?

BONUS IDEA If young people don't know each other's names well, pause every time after everyone is touching a lily pad so that the members on the same lily pad can introduce themselves and learn each other's names.

Arm-in-Arm with Simon

FOCUS
Young people build community by playing this group version of Simon Says.

SPARKS TIE-IN
- Dance/movement
- Learning
- Sports/athletics

YOU WILL NEED
- A large area

ACTIVITY Have young people create a circle where everyone is standing. Then ask them to link arms so that everyone in the circle is connected.

Explain that you're going to play a game of Simon Says. You'll name an action. If you say, "Simon says" before the action, everyone needs to do the action without unlinking arms. If you don't say "Simon says" before the action, no one is supposed to move.

Say, "Simon says to touch your nose." Give young people time to do this. Then say, "Stick out your tongue."

Name other actions, one at a time, inserting "Simon says" in front of some of the directions, but not all of them. Here are some examples:

- Hop up and down three times.
- Get down on your knees.
- Wiggle your hips.
- Shake your head.
- Clap your hands.

- March in place.
- Put your right foot into the circle.
- Put your left foot in back of you.
- Run in place as fast as you can.

End the activity by saying, "Simon says to unlink your arms."

DISCUSSION QUESTIONS

- How was it to do these actions with your arms linked?
- What did you think of this adaptation of Simon Says? Why?
- What did you experience when someone made a mistake and moved when he or she shouldn't have?
- Why do we need to learn how to work together as one community?
- How else can we build community?

BONUS IDEA Ask for a volunteer to lead this game again. Instead of using "Simon Says," use the volunteer's name, such as "Alex says."

Group Alphabet

FOCUS

Young people work together to form letters of the alphabet without speaking.

SPARKS TIE-IN

- Dance/movement
- Engineering
- Leadership
- Learning

YOU WILL NEED

- A ball or skein of yarn
- Scissors
- A yardstick

ACTIVITY Create small groups of four or five young people. Give each group a 10-foot piece of yarn.

Explain that each group is going to work together silently. You're going to name a letter of the alphabet and each group is to work together without speaking and form that letter out of the piece of yarn.

Have groups start by creating the letter L. (This one is easier than other letters.) Then give them other letters, one at a time:

A

F

H

M

B

If you have three groups, give one group E, another N, and another D. Have them spell "end" to finish your game. If you have six groups, spell "the end." If you have another number of groups, choose a different word to spell.

DISCUSSION QUESTIONS

- What was it like to do this activity in silence?
- How did you figure out how to communicate with each other without speaking?
- Which letter was the most difficult to make? Why?
- Why is it important to work together and build community in our group?
- How else could we use yarn to build community?

BONUS IDEA Instead of every group forming the same letter, assign different groups different letters and spell out words, such as "group," "fun," "build," or "join."

Group Rubber Band

FOCUS
Young people build community by acting like a rubber band together.

SPARKS TIE-IN
- Dance/movement
- Sports/athletics

YOU WILL NEED
- A large area

ACTIVITY Have young people form a large circle and hold hands. Explain that you're going to act like a group rubber band.

Practice by having the group "stretch out," moving outward as far as it can without dropping hands. Then have the group "snap in," where the group continues to hold hands but comes in as close together as they can.

Ask for a volunteer to start the activity by shouting out the first action. Then others can periodically yell out "stretch out" or "snap in" randomly through the activity. The activity will then take on a life of its own as group members randomly yell out directions.

DISCUSSION QUESTIONS
- What did you think of this activity? Why?
- Which did you like better: stretching out or snapping in? Why?
- Did the activity ever get too chaotic and confusing? If so, when?
- Why is it important for our group to work together?
- How else can we learn to work together to build community?

BONUS IDEA Do the activity again by adding another action for the human rubber band, "break." Young people first stretch out as far as they can and then drop hands as they move farther out.

Picture Pass

FOCUS

Young people build community and work together to pass along a picture in a group.

SPARKS TIE-IN

- Creative arts
- Relationships
- Visual arts

YOU WILL NEED

- A stack of 8½" x 11" white paper
- A bunch of pencils

ACTIVITY Create small groups of six to seven young people. Have each group form a line where they are all facing one direction and the people in line can only see the person's back in front of them. Give the young people at the front and ends of the lines a piece of paper and a pencil.

Explain that each group will communicate by drawing a picture on the back of the person in front of them with their fingers. The goal is to send the same picture from the back to the front of the line.

Ask groups to be quiet. Ask the group members at the back of each line to draw a simple picture on the piece of paper with a pencil. Simple pictures could be a tree, a circle, a star, a stick person, a mug, or something else.

After that person has drawn the picture, he or she then traces the picture with his or her finger on the back of the person in front of him or her. That person then traces the same thing on the back of the person in front of him or her.

Continue up the line (without talking) to the first person in line. The first person in line then draws the picture that was traced on his or her back onto the paper with the pencil.

Give groups time to compare the picture on the paper at the back of the line with the picture that was drawn at the front of the line.

Then have groups scramble by having the first and last person in line join their lines in the middle. (That way each group will have a new first and last person in line.) Repeat the activity.

DISCUSSION QUESTIONS

- How did the two pictures compare?
- What makes some images easier to communicate than others?
- Why is it important to communicate well to build community in our group?
- How can our group work through our miscommunications?

BONUS IDEA Instead of drawing a picture, write a short word, such as "big," "eat," "jump," or "goal."

Silent Knots

FOCUS

Young people build community by untangling a group knot without speaking.

SPARKS TIE-IN

- Dance/movement
- Engineering

YOU WILL NEED

- A large area

ACTIVITY Have young people create a circle. Have them move closer together. Then have each person stretch out his or her left hand and grab the hand of another person. Then have each person stretch out his or her right hand and grab another free hand.

Explain that the group will work to untangle this group knot without letting go of anyone's hands and without speaking.

See what happens.

DISCUSSION QUESTIONS

- Did you ever think it was impossible to untangle the knot? If so, when? If not, why not?
- How did you learn to communicate with each other without speaking?

- Who stepped up as leaders?
- Why is it important to have a sense of strong group community in order to work together well?
- How could we adapt this activity to build community in another way?

BONUS IDEA Repeat the activity except allow group members to talk. Then debrief the two experiences.

Reporter on the Scene

49

Handout

FOCUS
Interview another person to find out more about him or her.

SPARKS TIE-IN
- Journalism
- Relationships
- Writing

Choose two questions from the following list. Then find one person to ask these two questions. Write down that person's name and his or her answers.

- Who do you live with?
- What pets do you have?
- Who do you admire?
- What are you most proud of?

- How do you spend your weekends?
- What is the biggest world problem today?
- What do you like best about school?
- What do you want to be when you grow up?

Name or person interviewed: _____

Answers to the questions:

People Around You

FOCUS

Get to know the people around you by having them sign the statement that's true for them.

SPARKS TIE-IN

- Journalism
- Relationships
- Writing

Have each person sign one of the squares below that fits him or her. If the square has multiple possibilities (such as "plays on a sports team"), have the person sign his or her name and then write the name of the sport. Find a different person for each square. If your group is smaller than the number of squares, you can have some people sign more than one square after each person has signed one.

Plays on a sports team	Likes to cook	Lives with only one parent	Has been to a camp	Has never had a cavity
Has visited a foreign country	Plays a musical instrument	Is a Boy or Girl Scout	Likes to read books	Has a brother
Has broken a bone	Has a sister	Has been to a concert	Has met someone famous	Likes to swim
Has a friend in the same neighborhood	Is required to do household chores	Likes spending time with a grandpa or grandma	Attends a synagogue, church, or mosque	Has a pet
Speaks more than one language	Attends a different school than you do	Gets an allowance	Has moved in the past three years	Likes to go camping

What Matters to Me; What Matters to You

51

Handout

FOCUS

Compare what matters to you with what matters to another person.

SPARKS TIE-IN

- Animals
- Comedy
- Relationships
- Serving, helping, volunteering

What matters to you? Answer the questions in the "What Matters to Me" column on page 81. Write a checkmark by one answer: either "a little," "some" or "a lot."

When you finish, find another person and ask him or her to answer the questions in the "What Matters to You" column on page 81.

Afterward, ask yourself these questions:

- What matters a lot to both of you?
- How many items did you agree on?

Handout

Activity	What Matters to Me			What Matters to You		
	A Little	Some	A Lot	A Little	Some	A Lot
1. Listening to music						
2. Laughing						
3. Surfing the Internet						
4. Spending time with a friend						
5. Reading						
6. Texting						
7. Spending time with animals or a pet						
8. Doing homework						
9. Playing a sport						
10. Helping others						
11. Spending time with my family						
12. Singing or playing an instrument						
13. Talking on the phone						
14. Creating art						
15. Watching a funny movie or TV show						

CHAPTER 5

Acting-Together Activities

Once a group has built a strong sense of community, it needs to go even deeper. The group needs to learn how to act as a single unit and to do so well. The need for this type of teamwork is most apparent in team sports, such as soccer or football, yet every class and group needs to act together in order for the entire group and for every individual to succeed. ▶▶

Group Spin

FOCUS

Young people work together to keep a flying disc spinning for as long as possible.

SPARKS TIE-IN

- Engineering
- Relationships
- Teaching/coaching

YOU WILL NEED

- 1 flying disc (or Frisbee)
- An uncarpeted floor
- A timer or stopwatch

ACTIVITY Have young people form a circle. Ask for a volunteer who is good at spinning a flying disc on its side on the floor to step into the middle of the circle.

Explain that you're going to set a timer and see how long the group can keep the flying disc spinning. The volunteer will start and once the flying disc is spinning, he or she will call out another group member's name. That person will then enter the circle and take over the first person.

The second person keeps the flying disc spinning and calls out the name of another group member, who enters the circle and takes over. Continue this process as long as possible. See how long your group can keep the disc spinning.

Encourage group members to call out ideas for how to keep the flying disc spinning. Usually someone (or a group of people) can suggest ways to do this. They can become the head coaches for this activity.

DISCUSSION QUESTIONS

- What was most difficult about keeping the disc spinning?
- How did you smoothly transfer responsibility for keeping the flying disc without letting the disc fall?
- What techniques did you discover would help keep the disc spinning?
- Why does it matter for our group to learn how to work together?
- How else can we learn to work together better?

BONUS IDEA Create a larger circle. Add a second flying disc. See if your group can work together to keep two discs spinning.

Table for All

FOCUS
Young people get together to talk and listen to each other.

SPARKS TIE-IN
* Learning
* Relationships

YOU WILL NEED
* A large area

ACTIVITY Have young people spread out. Explain that you're going to call out "Table for" and then a number, such as two or three. When young people hear that number, they need to form a group with that many people in it. If one or more people are left over, these people can join one of the groups, but only one person can join each group.

Once the groups are made, you will then give them something to talk about.

Begin by calling out, "Table for two." Once pairs are created, have young people discuss what they like to drink best and why.

When they finish talking, ask them to spread out again. Call out "Table for three." Once groups of three are formed, have young people discuss what their favorite meal main course is and why.

When they finish talking, ask them to spread out again. Call out "Table for four." Once groups of four are formed, have young people discuss what their favorite vegetable is and why.

When they finish talking, ask them to spread out again. Call out "Table for six." Once groups of six are formed, have young people discuss what their favorite fruit is and why.

When they finish talking, ask them to spread out again. Call out "Table for eight." Once groups of eight are formed, have young people discuss what their favorite grain is and why.

When they finish talking, ask them to spread out again. Call out "Table for all." Once one large group has gathered together, have young people discuss what their favorite dessert is and why.

DISCUSSION QUESTIONS

- What did you like best about talking with different group members?
- Why does it matter to listen to other group members?
- Why does it matter to talk to other group members?
- Why do talking together and listening to each other help us work together better?
- How else can learn to listen to each other better?

BONUS IDEA Do the activity again with other topics, such as "What is your favorite activity to do?" or "Where is your favorite place to go?" or "What's your favorite music (or TV show or movie)?"

Double Up!

FOCUS

Young people learn how to move together in unique ways.

SPARKS TIE-IN

- Dance/movement
- Relationships
- Sports/athletics

YOU WILL NEED

- A large area

ACTIVITY Have young people spread out. Explain that you're going to do an activity where group members learn how to work together.

Have everyone find a partner. If you have an extra person, form one group of three.

Have partners figure out a unique way to move around your area together, such as skipping together, marching, hopping on one foot, taking giant steps, shuffling their feet, or some other creative motion. Give pairs time to choose a movement. Then have them start doing the movement.

Once pairs are moving, call out, "Double up!" Encourage each pair to find another pair to "double up" with so that they're now working in groups of fours.

Encourage the groups to find a new movement that none of the members have done before. Then once they figure that out, have them do that movement together.

Once all the groups are moving, give them a few seconds before saying, "Double up!" Keep doing the activity until you have just one large group that will need to work together to choose a new action.

DISCUSSION QUESTIONS

- How did you get members of a group to all work together for this activity?
- What kind of group do you like working in best: small groups or a large group? Why?
- Why does it matter to listen for ideas from other group members?
- Why is it important for groups to have leaders and followers?
- How else can we work together?

BONUS IDEA If you have a large group, play "Triple up!" or "Quadruple up!"

Group Song

FOCUS

Young people sing a song together in an unusual way.

SPARKS TIE-IN

- Creative arts
- Music
- Relationships

YOU WILL NEED

- A large area

ACTIVITY If you have 10 young people or fewer, do this as one group. If you have more than 10 present, create two or three groups so that each group has no more than 10 people.

Have groups sit or stand in a circle. Explain that you're going to sing a song as a group but in an unusual way. Each group will sing "Twinkle, Twinkle, Little Star." One person will start, and the group members will take turns singing around the circle moving clockwise. The trick, however, is that each person can sing only one word and the circle members need to keep in rhythm as they sing the song.

Thus, the person who starts will sing, "Twinkle." The person sitting next to that person going clockwise sings, "Twinkle." The next person sings, "Little." The next person sings, "Star." The circle group continues in this way around the circle until the entire song has been sung.

Once young people understand how this works, sing the song.

DISCUSSION QUESTIONS

- What did you think of this activity before we did it? After?
- What was it like singing one word in front of the group?
- How did this activity show how we work together?
- What can help us work together better?

BONUS IDEA Try other common, simple songs, such as "Mary Had a Little Lamb," "Baa, Baa, Black Sheep," "Row, Row, Row Your Boat," or "The Bear Went Over the Mountain." Or ask young people for song ideas.

Locked Out

56

FOCUS
Young people experience what it's like not to be part of your group.

SPARKS TIE-IN
- Dance/movement
- Relationships
- Sports/athletics

YOU WILL NEED
- A large area

ACTIVITY Ask for two volunteers. Explain that these two people will be "locked out" of your group.

Have the rest of your group members form a tight circle by standing close together. Explain that the two outsiders who are locked out of the group will do anything they can (within reason and with safety in mind) to get into the tight circle. (If you have some strong kids in your group, you might want to suggest that young people yell out "foul" if someone is hurting them or getting too rough. If anyone hears the word "foul," it means to take the physical activity down a notch or two.)

Do the activity. See how it goes for the two volunteers who are locked out.

Then repeat the activity with two different volunteers as the outsiders.

Consider repeating the activity until everyone has had the chance to experience what it was like to be "locked out" of the larger group.

DISCUSSION QUESTIONS
- How did it feel to be locked out of the group?
- How did it feel to be part of the larger group that worked hard to keep some people out?
- Based on your experience with this activity, how can we work together better?
- Why is it important to include everyone in our group?
- How can our group be more welcoming to newcomers or other people who may feel like outsiders in our group?

BONUS IDEA Repeat the activity but have the goal of integrating those who are locked out into the middle of the group.

Draw Together

FOCUS
Young people tap into their creativity and draw a picture together.

SPARKS TIE-IN
- Creative arts
- Relationships
- Visual arts

YOU WILL NEED
- 1 piece of newsprint (or another type of large paper) for every five young people
- 1 washable marker for each young person (in as many different colors as possible)

ACTIVITY Create small groups of five young people. (You also can have a group of three or seven since you want odd-numbered groups.) Give each group a piece of newsprint. Give each young person a marker. Ideally, each small-group member would have a different colored marker.

Explain that each group is going to do one drawing. No one needs to be an expert at drawing. This activity is more about working together than about having artistic talent.

Have each small group sit in a circle and choose one person to start the activity. That person will tell the person on his or her left what to draw. It needs to be a single item. For example, the first person may say, "car" or "building" or "dog."

Continue the activity moving clockwise. After the second person draws the item on the newsprint, the third person then tells the fourth person something to draw that will embellish the first drawing. For example, if the person drew a dog, the third person may say, "the dog has a broken leg." The fourth person then draws that.

Then the fifth person tells the first person another embellishment to add to the drawing. For example, that person may say, "The dog is chasing a cat." A cat is then added to the picture.

Continue in this manner until each group has gone around the circle at least twice. Each person should have had a turn to draw and a turn to tell another person what to draw.

DISCUSSION QUESTIONS

- What did you think of this activity before we did it? After?
- What did you enjoy more: thinking up something to draw or drawing it? Why?
- What did you think of your finished group drawing? Why?
- How can an activity like this help us work together better?
- How else can we discover how to work together better?

BONUS IDEA Try doing this activity quickly and with the idea of being as ridiculous as possible. Expect giggling.

Ups and Downs

FOCUS

Young people tell their ups and downs from your time together as a group.

SPARKS TIE-IN

- Learning
- Relationships
- Solving social problems

YOU WILL NEED

- A large area

ACTIVITY At the end of your group time together, make time to do "Ups and Downs." This activity is a great way to debrief your time together and get young people to give you feedback on how your activity or group went.

Have young people gather in a circle. Go around the circle and ask each person to name one "down" (or something they didn't like or found boring) from your time together. Then once everyone has said one "down," go around the circle and have each person say one "up" (or something they really enjoyed) from your time together.

DISCUSSION QUESTIONS

- What was easier for you to think of: an up or a down? Why?

- How did this activity help you think about our time together?
- Why is it important to give feedback from time to time?
- How can getting feedback about our group improve the way our group works?
- How else can we provide feedback?

BONUS IDEA Consider doing this activity on a regular basis. Some groups do it every time they meet. Others do it three or four times during their season or quarter.

Moving Blob

FOCUS
Young people move together in one large blob.

SPARKS TIE-IN
- Dance/movement
- Relationships
- Sports/athletics

YOU WILL NEED
- A 25'–50' piece of yarn (depending on your group size)
- Scissors
- A large area

ACTIVITY Explain that your entire group is going to do an activity together. The group will form a large "blob" by standing as close together as possible. You'll then tie a piece of yarn around the blob at waist height.

Once you have a piece of yarn around the entire group, cut it and tie it.

Then have the blob start to move. If possible, create a course for the blob to move in. Encourage the blob to move slowly so that no one gets hurt. Then see what happens as it moves.

DISCUSSION QUESTIONS
- How did you feel you were working together?

- When did you feel you were not working together? What happened?
- Who became the leaders? Why do you think that happened?
- Why does it matter to do an activity like this?
- How else can we practice working together?

BONUS IDEA Some groups really enjoy this activity. If yours does, create more challenging places for the blob to move, such as up or down stairs (the blob will need to move very carefully so no one falls) or around or over an obstacle.

Everyone Belongs

FOCUS

Each young person in the group writes his or her name to show that everyone belongs in your group.

SPARKS TIE-IN

- Creative arts
- Relationships
- Visual arts

YOU WILL NEED

- 1 piece of poster board (or another type of large paper)
- 1 washable marker for each young person (in as many different colors as possible)
- Masking or painter's tape

ACTIVITY Explain that in your group everyone belongs. Hang up the poster board in a prominent place in your group area.

Give each young person a marker. Have young people take turns (in twos or threes) writing their names on the poster board. Make sure every young person in your group writes his or her name.

DISCUSSION QUESTIONS

- How did it feel to write your name on this poster board?

- If we kept this poster board hanging in front of our group every time we met, how would you feel? Why?
- Why is it important for each person to feel like he or she belongs to our group?
- What else can we do with our names to help learn each other's names?

BONUS IDEA Make this activity more of an art project by giving young people time to outline their names and draw shapes or designs inside of their names.

You and Your Favorite Activity

61

FOCUS
Let others know what your favorite activity is.

SPARKS TIE-IN
- All of them

Write your name: _____

Write your favorite activity: _____

Write your favorite activity in the space above. Then move around the group and have each group member read your name and favorite activity and then sign his or her name on this paper below. (If you're shy, find someone who is more outgoing to be your partner for this activity.) Get every group member's signature.

How Does Our Group Rate?

FOCUS

Rate our group according to its strengths and weaknesses.

SPARKS TIE-IN

- Learning
- Relationships
- Solving social problems

Rate our group by circling one word that describes how well you agree with each statement on the chart.

Ask yourself these questions:

- Of statements 1–10, which one does the group need more work at? Why?
- Of statements 1–10, which one is the group best at? Why?

How Does Our Group Rate?
continued

Handout

Statement	Absolutely	Mostly Yes	Yes and No	No
1. Our group is good at listening to group members.	Absolutely	Mostly Yes	Yes and No	No
2. Our group is good at helping me feel included.	Absolutely	Mostly Yes	Yes and No	No
3. Our group members work well together.	Absolutely	Mostly Yes	Yes and No	No
4. Our group is fun to be a part of.	Absolutely	Mostly Yes	Yes and No	No
5. I'm proud of our group.	Absolutely	Mostly Yes	Yes and No	No
6. I feel cared for by members of this group.	Absolutely	Mostly Yes	Yes and No	No
7. I feel cared for by the adult leaders of this group.	Absolutely	Mostly Yes	Yes and No	No
8. I look forward to coming to this group.	Absolutely	Mostly Yes	Yes and No	No
9. I would recommend this group to other people I know.	Absolutely	Mostly Yes	Yes and No	No
10. I trust other group members.	Absolutely	Mostly Yes	Yes and No	No

Group Connections

FOCUS

Learn the names of other people in our group.

SPARKS TIE-IN

- Relationships

As a group, we are all connected. In the top puzzle piece, write your first name. Then move around the group and find another group member who will write his or her first name on a different puzzle piece. (You can also write your name on that person's puzzle.)

Continue finding group members to sign your puzzle until every piece has a name.

Ask yourself these questions:

- How are we all connected as part of this group?
- Why does it matter to know that we're connected?

CHAPTER 6

Working Independently Activities

Although group process and teamwork are essential, it's also vital for each individual in your class, group, or team to be able to work independently and meet individual goals. With so many technological gadgets, kids today often don't know how to work independently. They're used to being entertained. The activities in this chapter encourage kids to learn the essential skills on how to work on their own and how to work well independently. ▸▸

Your View of Nature

FOCUS

Young people create a nature journal to get more in touch with the outdoors.

SPARKS TIE-IN

- Nature, ecology, environment
- Outdoor life
- Visual arts
- Writing

YOU WILL NEED

- 10 pieces of 8½" x 11" white paper for each person
- Stapler
- 3–5 washable markers for each person
- 1 pencil with an eraser for each person
- An outdoor area

ACTIVITY Choose a day when you can be outside comfortably. Ideally, choose a place where kids can view nature, such as a park, a nature center, or a wooded area of a public place. Before you do this activity, staple 10 pieces of paper together to create a journal for each person.

Give each young person the 10-page journal, some markers, and a pencil. Have young people create a cover for their journal by writing the name for their journal and their name, and then decorating their journal with drawings of nature.

Then explain that you're going to spend time outside and that young people are to keep a journal of their view of nature. Young people can either write about what they see and experience, draw pictures of what they see, or do a combination of both drawing and writing.

Give young people time to explore the outdoors safely. Encourage them to draw or write about what they see: plants, animals, birds, trees, and so on. Explain that there is no wrong way to do this. They can create a new page for each new thing they see.

Once everyone finishes, ask for volunteers to show a page or two from their journals.

DISCUSSION QUESTIONS

- What was your first reaction to creating a nature journal? Why?
- What did you discover about nature while we were outside?
- Why does it matter what your perspective about nature is?
- How else can we spend time outdoors in nature?

BONUS IDEA Create a classroom nature journal where you photocopy one to two pages of each person's journal and combine it into one class journal.

On the Map

FOCUS

Young people discover how to read maps.

SPARKS TIE-IN

- Learning
- Nature, ecology, environment
- Reading

YOU WILL NEED

- Printouts of your state map (free from p6.secure.hostingprod.com/@newatlas .com/ssl/dlmaps/downloadable_state_maps.php), one for each young person
- Lots of washable markers in different colors

ACTIVITY Give each young person a copy of your state map and a number of markers.

Ask them to first outline your state. If they have trouble, you can help them out. Explain that usually state boundary lines are shown by a line that has dashes and dots, by a river, or a major highway.

Then have young people color in the major bodies of water within the state. Next, they should circle the largest cities within the state. Point out that the larger the type size on the map, the larger the city. If your state has a major river, such as the Mississippi, Ohio, Arkansas, Colorado, the Rio Grande, or another, have them follow the path of the river with a colored marker.

Give young people time to discover other interesting things about your state.

For example, some may recognize certain major highways or major counties. Some may even find the name of their city on the map.

Once everyone finishes, ask for volunteers to talk about what they discovered.

DISCUSSION QUESTIONS

- What did you discover about our state through this activity?
- How can studying a map help us learn more about our state?
- Why is it important to become familiar with our state?
- How else can we learn about our state?

BONUS IDEA Print out maps of all 50 states and assign each state to a different young person. Have them learn more about the state they have been assigned and then share it with your group.

Another Way

FOCUS

Young people create art and learn how to develop something new from their art.

SPARKS TIE-IN

- Creative arts
- Entrepreneur
- Visual arts

YOU WILL NEED

- 5–7 self-stick notes (3" x 3") for each young person
- 1 pen for each young person
- 1 piece of 8½" x 11" white paper for each young person

ACTIVITY Have young people place the self-stick notes next to each other on a piece of paper until the self-stick notes touch. Then ask them to draw a picture across all the self-stick notes with a pen.

Once everyone finishes, have young people remove the self-stick notes from the paper. Have them turn over the paper and use it in a different direction. (For example, those who have already used the paper vertically as 8½ inches wide by 11 inches tall should now turn the paper so that it's 11 inches wide and 8½ inches tall.)

Have the young people place the self-stick notes on the paper but in a different order. Once they've placed all the self-stick notes, what do they see?

Explain that they just completed an exercise in creativity and entrepreneurship. Say that entrepreneurs are people who create things: as artists, businesspeople, or anyone in any field or subject. Entrepreneurs look at things differently than other people and create something new—just like they did in this activity.

DISCUSSION QUESTIONS

- What do you see in your new arrangement of self-stick notes?
- What would happen if you moved the self-stick notes again?
- Why is it important to try new things?
- How else can we become creative?

BONUS IDEA Have the group create a class picture by having young people choose one of their self-stick notes to add to one large picture.

Computer Game Exploration

FOCUS

Young people discover which educational computer games they're drawn to.

SPARKS TIE-IN

- Computers
- Learning

YOU WILL NEED

- A computer with Internet access for each young person (or each pair of young people)

ACTIVITY Find a bank of computers to use at a school media center, public library, or local organization.

Have young people visit the PBS Kids Zoom educational game site at pbskids.org/zoom/games. *Zoom* is an educational show that's created by kids for kids.

Encourage kids to try different games, paying attention to which ones they're attracted to, which ones they're not, and what their experience was like with their games. Give kids time to play a number of different games.

DISCUSSION QUESTIONS

- Which game did you start with? Why?
- Which game did you avoid? Why?
- How do you decide which computer games to try?
- What can computer games teach you about yourself and your interests?
- Why is it important to know which computer games you enjoy playing?
- What else can you learn from computer games?

BONUS IDEA At the PBS Kids Zoom website, click on "Printables" or "Parents & Teachers" for more activities for your group.

Book Cover Design

FOCUS
Young people create a book cover based on one of their interests.

SPARKS TIE-IN

- Creative arts
- Reading
- Visual arts
- Writing

YOU WILL NEED

- 1 piece of 8½" x 11" white paper for each young person
- 3–5 washable markers in a variety of colors for each young person
- Examples of colorful, attractive book covers that appeal to this age group (optional)

ACTIVITY Give each young person a piece of paper and three to five markers. Have them identify one interest, activity, or sport that they really enjoy.

Explain that each person will create a book cover based on the interest, activity, or sport they chose. They need to decide on a catchy title and then draw a picture to illustrate the activity. If you have examples of colorful book covers, show them to the young people.

Give young people time to create their book covers. When they finish, ask for volunteers to show the group what they created.

DISCUSSION QUESTIONS

- How did you decide which activity, interest, or sport to illustrate?
- Which was easier for you: thinking up a book title or illustrating your cover? Why?
- How often do you pick a book to read based on what the cover looks like?
- Why does it matter what's on a book cover?
- How can our favorite book covers tell us something about ourselves?

BONUS IDEA Display all the book covers. Or consider having young people create book covers for their favorite books.

People You Admire

FOCUS
Young people identify two people they admire and name characteristics about them.

SPARKS TIE-IN:
- Family
- Leadership
- Relationships

YOU WILL NEED
- 1 piece of 8½" x 11" white paper for each young person
- 1 pen or pencil for each young person

ACTIVITY Give each young person a piece of paper and a pen or pencil. Have them write their name on the top of their paper. Then have them draw a line down the center of the paper so that they have two columns.

Have them think of two adults they admire. They can be immediate family members, coaches, teachers, neighbors, extended family members, club leaders, music teachers, or other adults they know and look up to. Have them write the name of one adult at the top of the left-hand column and the name of the other adult on the top of the right-hand column.

Give young people time to identify five characteristics they admire about each adult. Explain that since everyone is different, the lists most likely will be different as well. If young people have trouble identifying positive characteristics, do a group brainstorm and list all their ideas on a chalkboard, white board, or newsprint.

DISCUSSION QUESTIONS

- How do you know the people you admire?
- Which characteristics did your two adults have in common?
- Which characteristics were different about your two adults?
- Why is it important for adults to be role models?
- How else can we learn about role models?

BONUS IDEA Collect all of the young people's papers, photocopy them, and then compile them into booklets to distribute to the group. This allows young people to learn more about the admirable adults their peers look up to.

Advocacy List

FOCUS
Young people identify a social justice problem and list ways they can help.

SPARKS TIE-IN

- Advocacy
- Serving, helping, volunteering
- Solving social problems

YOU WILL NEED

- 1 piece of 8½" x 11" white paper for each young person
- 1 pen or pencil for each young person
- 1 large sheet of newsprint
- 1 washable marker
- Masking or painter's tape

ACTIVITY Give each young person a piece of paper and a pen or pencil. Have them write their name on the top of their paper.

Explain that there are a lot of problems facing our community and world today. As a group, brainstorm ideas of social problems, such as pollution, global warming, and poverty. List all the ideas on a piece of newsprint to display in front of the group.

Explain that each person will choose a social problem that he or she is very concerned about. It's okay if more than one person chooses the same problem. The social problem they choose, however, should be something where they feel their actions can make a difference. For example, some kids may find the issue of global warming overwhelming and won't have specific ideas of what they can do, but others may be able to identify specific actions they can take toward this problem.

Give young people time to identify a social problem and list three actions they can take to make a difference with that problem. For example, someone may choose the problem of poverty and decide these three things to do about it: 1. Save money to give to an organization that helps the poor; 2. Donate used clothing to the poor; and 3. Eat only rice one day to see what it feels like to have little food.

DISCUSSION QUESTIONS

- Which social problem did you choose? Why?
- How easy or hard was it to name ways to do something about this problem?
- Which idea that you listed will you do first?
- Why does it matter that individuals make a difference in solving social problems?
- What else can we do to solve social problems?

BONUS IDEA Consider creating a wall display that lists all the social problems the young people chose along with one action they plan to do to make a difference.

Ice-Cube Competition

FOCUS

Young people explore different ways to melt an ice cube.

SPARKS TIE-IN

- Building and design
- Engineering
- Learning
- Nature, ecology, environment

YOU WILL NEED

- 1 ice cube for each young person
- 1 paper cup for each young person
- 1 pen for each young person
- A variety of materials: newspaper, masking tape, aluminum foil, rubber bands, waxed paper, small pieces of cardboard, small pieces of cloth, paper clips, pennies, tissue paper, facial tissues, paper towels, small pieces of bubble wrap, small plastic bags, salt, duct tape, cotton balls, and so on

ACTIVITY Give each young person a paper cup and a pen. Have them each write their name on the bottom of their cups. Keep the ice cubes frozen until you're ready to start.

Explain that you're going to have a competition to see which method can keep an ice cube from melting the fastest. Show young people the variety of materials. Explain that each person needs to do something different. For example, one person may wrap the ice cube in newspaper and then place it in the cup. Another person may put the ice cube in a plastic bag and then put it in the cup. Another person may surround the ice cube with pennies inside the cup. Have young people each choose a different method. They can also combine methods, such as putting cotton balls on the bottom of the cup and then placing the ice cube inside of a plastic bag.

Have each person get his or her materials ready. As soon as everyone is set, give each person an ice cube. Then do another activity while you wait. Depending on the methods chosen, an ice cube could stay frozen for 1 hour or 15 hours.

DISCUSSION QUESTIONS

- Why did you choose the materials that you did?
- How much do you enjoy doing science projects like this one?
- Why do you think some materials kept the ice solid longer than others?
- Why is it important to experiment?
- What other experiments could we try?

BONUS IDEA Have young people brainstorm other materials they could use to keep an ice cube from melting. Then try their ideas.

Sponge Painting Creation

FOCUS
Young people make a sponge painting.

SPARKS TIE-IN
- Creative arts
- Visual arts

YOU WILL NEED
- Liquid tempera paint in a variety of colors
- 1–3 sheets of newspaper for each young person
- 1 piece of 8½" x 11" paper for each young person
- Sponges
- Scissors
- 1 clothespin for each young person
- 1 paper cup for each young person
- 1 paint shirt for each young person
- Water and paper towels for cleanup
- Plastic garbage bags for cleanup

ACTIVITY Cut sponges to a size of one by two inches. Give each young person a paint shirt, newspaper to cover his or her desk or table, a piece of white paper, a sponge, a clothespin, and a paper cup.

Explain that you're going to do sponge painting. Have young people take their clothespin and firmly place the sponge inside of the clothespin's clasp. Demonstrate how they will hold the clothespin, dip the sponge into their cup (which will eventually hold paint), and then dab their paper to create a picture.

Once young people have their paint shirts on, have them choose one paint color, and then pour some tempera paint into their cups. Explain that they are to paint with only that one color. You don't need to give young people much paint since the sponges are small. It's always easier to add more paint to a cup than throw out a lot of paint afterward.

Give young people time to sponge paint their pictures. When they finish, have them throw out the sponges connected to clothespins and their cups. Leave their paintings on the newspaper to dry.

DISCUSSION QUESTIONS
- What surprised you about painting in this way?
- What would make this painting technique even more interesting to you?
- Why is it important to try different kinds of art activities?
- What other type of art activity could we do? Why?

BONUS IDEA Have young people paint something based on a theme. You could focus on caring for the environment, and young people could sponge paint trees, flowers, and nature scenes. Or you could focus on animals, sports, the arts, or some other topic.

Your Top 10

Handout

73

FOCUS

Identify your 10 favorite items and examine what they reveal about you.

SPARKS TIE-IN

* All of them

If you could keep only 10 items, what would you keep? List them below.

1.

2.

3.

4.

5.

6.

7.

8.

9.

10.

Ask yourself these questions:

* What do the 10 items tell you about yourself?
* What do the 10 items tell you about your interests and sparks?

Your Favorite Places

FOCUS
Name your favorite places and identify why they mean a lot to you.

SPARKS TIE-IN
- Living in a specific way
- Spirituality

For many people, going to a favorite place helps them to feel relaxed and at home with who they are. For some people, a favorite place is also a sacred place. Think about three favorite places. They could be a home (or a room in a home), a special place in nature, a place of worship, a favorite tree, or another place that you just love. Then write about your three favorite places.

Ask yourself these questions:
- What does your favorite place do for you?
- What makes your favorite place special to you?
- How do you know when you've discovered a favorite place?

Brick by Brick, Row by Row

75

Handout

FOCUS

Identify words that represent service and volunteering.

SPARKS TIE-IN

- Nature, ecology, environment
- Serving, helping, volunteering
- Solving social problems

Insert the following service action words into the brick wall below to show how service is built brick by brick, row by row. Each of the missing words appears horizontally on the brick wall. Only the word SERVICE appears vertically.

4-Letter Words			5-Letter Words			7-Letter Words		
Care	Give	Help		Visit		Collect	Recycle	Support

		S	__	__	__	__	__	__
	__	E	__					
__	__	R	__					
__	__	V	__					
	__	I		__				
		C	__	__	__			
	__	E	__	__				

Ask yourself these questions::

- When have you helped others?
- How do other people you know help others?
- How can you help others?

Answer Key: Words (in order from top to bottom): Support, Recycle, Care, Give, Visit, Collect, Help.

CHAPTER 7

Breaking-Up-Boredom Activities

This happens too often with groups: Your group was working together well when suddenly you lost some or most of them. Some group members got bored with the activity or their minds wandered off. The activities in this chapter break up boredom by getting kids moving and doing something different for a short time. These activities help kids to refocus so that they're ready to go back to the activity that you were doing before you lost them. ▶▶

One-Minute Cram

FOCUS

Young people learn as much as they can about a partner in one minute.

SPARKS TIE-IN

- Learning
- Speech

YOU WILL NEED

- A timer or clock that records seconds and minutes
- A large area

ACTIVITY Have each young person find a partner. If there is an extra person, ask an adult leader to pair up with the young person. Have partners spread out throughout the area.

Explain that you're going to do a quick activity. You'll give partners one minute to learn as much as they can about their partner. After one minute, you'll stop and then quiz partners to see how much they learned about each other.

Give partners one minute to learn as much as they can about each other.

When one minute has passed, ask partners to stop. Then have them sit back to back so they cannot see each other. Ask the following questions one at a time; tell young people to raise their hand if they know the answer. Ask these questions:

- What kind of shoes is your partner wearing?
- Is your partner wearing a long-sleeve or a short-sleeve shirt?
- What color eyes does your partner have?
- What color shirt is your partner wearing?
- Does your partner part his or her hair? If so, on which side?

When someone raises his or her hand to answer the question aloud to the group, have the partner then say "right" or "wrong."

DISCUSSION QUESTIONS

- Before I had you sit back to back, did you think one minute was long enough to learn a lot about your partner? Why or why not?
- Were you surprised by the questions I asked? Why or why not?
- Why does it matter to pay attention to what's going on with others in our group?

- Why is it important to get to know other group members?
- How else can we get to know group members?

BONUS IDEA To give young people the chance to share what they learned during their one-minute cram, have volunteers stand up and give a couple of facts about their partner. This helps group members learn even more about each other.

Megafast Fire Drill

FOCUS
Young people release some steam by moving around the room.

SPARKS TIE-IN
- Dance/movement
- Sports/athletics
- Outdoor life (if you do this outside)

YOU WILL NEED
- A large area

ACTIVITY Have young people stand up when they're getting restless. Explain that you're going to do a quick activity. When you yell "Megafast Fire Drill," you want everyone to start running around the area clockwise. When you yell "stop," everyone should stop.

Yell, "Megafast fire drill!" After about 10 to 15 seconds, yell "stop." Let kids rest for a few seconds before yelling "Megafast fire drill" again.

End the activity by yelling, "stop."

DISCUSSION QUESTIONS
- What did you think of this activity? Why?
- Why is it important to run around sometimes?
- What do you usually do when you get restless or antsy?
- Why is it important to use up some of your restless energy from time to time?
- How else could we get rid of restless energy?

BONUS IDEA Play "Forward fire drill" and "Backward fire drill." Have young people run clockwise in the area whenever you say "Forward fire drill" and counterclockwise when you say "Backward fire drill."

Comic Strip Ending

FOCUS
Young people create the final panel of a newspaper comic strip.

SPARKS TIE-IN
- Comedy
- Creative arts
- Visual arts
- Writing

YOU WILL NEED
- A daily newspaper with the comic strips
- 1 pencil for each young person
- 1 piece of 8½" x 11" white paper for each young person
- Scissors

ACTIVITY Before you do this activity, cut out comic strips out of a daily newspaper. Cut off the last panel of each one (since you'll ask each young person to create his or her ending).

Give each young person a comic strip, a pencil, and a piece of paper. Explain that each person received a comic strip that is missing the last panel. Encourage young people to draw and write the last panel of their comic strip.

When young people finish, have them read their comic strips aloud and show what they drew.

DISCUSSION QUESTIONS:
- What was it like to finish someone else's comic strip?
- How often do you read comic strips? Why?
- What are your favorite comic strips?

- Why does it matter to create something new from time to time?
- How else could we be creative?

BONUS IDEA Give each young person the final panel of the comic strip from the newspaper to compare their ending with the cartoonist's ending. Emphasize that one ending isn't better than the other.

Balloon Blastoff

FOCUS
Young people experiment with different ways to launch a balloon through a room.

SPARKS TIE-IN
- Building and design
- Engineering

YOU WILL NEED
- A large floor area
- A balloon for each young person
- A rubber band for each young person
- A straw for each young person (half of them bendy straws and half straight straws)
- Scissors

ACTIVITY Give each young person a balloon, a rubber band, and a straw. Make sure half of the young people have straws that are bendy straws and the other half have straight straws.

Explain that the group is doing an experiment to see how balloons move around with their straw launchers. (They'll move sideways across a floor, not up.) Have young people inflate their balloons and place a straw into the opening of the balloon without letting out any air. (If anyone is using a bendy straw, make sure they place the shorter end of the bendy straw at the mouth of the balloon.)

Then have them secure the straw into the balloon by wrapping a rubber band around the balloon where the straw enters the balloon, again without letting out any air.

Walk around the group with a scissors. Cut off different amounts of the straws so all of the straws are different lengths. For example, cut off one inch from the end of one young person's straw, two inches from of another, three inches off another, and so on. Make sure you do this for both the straight and bendy straws so that you can compare results.

Then begin a countdown; at the end the young people will let go of their balloons and see what happens.

DISCUSSION QUESTIONS
- What happened when you let go of your balloon?
- Why do you think balloons did different things?
- Why is it important to try new things?
- What else could we try to make balloons move?

BONUS IDEA Inflate a balloon. Tie the end of it. Then have young people bat it into the air. See how many times they can bat the balloon without the balloon falling to the ground. Then challenge them further by adding a second or even a third balloon.

Your Family, Your Life

FOCUS
Young people talk about their families and their lives with other group members.

SPARKS TIE-IN
- Family
- Relationships

YOU WILL NEED
- A large area
- Music and speakers

ACTIVITY Have young people spread out in a large area. Explain that you'll play music. Whenever they hear music, they need to move around the area. When the music stops, they need to find a partner nearby. (If there is an extra person, one group can have three people in it.)

Play the music while the young people move around. After a few moments, stop the music. Once young people have a partner, have them briefly talk about who lives with them.

Then play the music again while young people move around the area. After a bit, stop the music. Have pairs talk about one of these topics:

- What is your bedroom like?
- How long have you lived where you live?
- What pets does your family have or what pet would you like to have?
- What do you like to do with your family?
- Which family members who don't live with you do you enjoy spending time with?
- Has your family ever taken a trip? If so, where?
- How does your family celebrate birthdays?

Choose a different topic for pairs to discuss every time the music stops.

DISCUSSION QUESTIONS
- What interesting fact did you learn about someone?
- How often did you find you had something in common with the other group members?
- Why does it matter to know a bit about the families of our group members?
- How else can we learn about each other's family?

BONUS IDEA Create a question box. Give each young person a piece of paper and pencil. Have each write a question he or she would like to ask group members. Go through the papers before reading them aloud as questions (to screen anything that may be inappropriate). Young people often have great ideas for insightful questions to ask.

I Spy

FOCUS

Young people work out their wiggles by going outside to spy different objects.

SPARKS TIE-IN

- Nature, ecology, environment
- Outdoor life
- Sports/athletics

YOU WILL NEED

- An area outside

ACTIVITY Go outside as a group. Play "I Spy" by naming different areas or objects you see outside while also naming a way you want young people to get there. For example, say, "I spy a running tree." This tells young people to run to a tree.

Here are some other suggestions:

- Walking bush
- Skipping outhouse
- Jumping playground
- Marching flowers
- Zigzagging trash can
- Somersaulting grass
- Hopping curb

DISCUSSION QUESTIONS

- What did you discover about the outdoor area?
- Which action, such as marching, skipping, or something else, did you enjoy best?
- Why is it important to move our bodies from time to time?
- What else could we add next time?

BONUS IDEA To help young people get to know group members better, play "I Spy" where you name one of the group members and then everyone forms a circle around that person.

Put a Lid on It

FOCUS

Young people privately identify their negative feelings and then place boundaries on them.

SPARKS TIE-IN

- Building and design
- Creative arts
- Visual arts

YOU WILL NEED

- A shoebox (or some type of box with a lid) for each young person
- 5 pieces of 8½" x 11" white paper for each young person
- Lots of washable markers

Caution: Some young people may be dealing with extremely difficult situations and feelings. Be aware that this activity may bring up feelings that some kids have suppressed. Be compassionate but also be clear about appropriate ways to act and express feelings.

ACTIVITY Explain that sometimes our feelings make us antsy, which makes it hard to concentrate. Instead of suppressing those feelings, we're going to do an activity to help get those feelings out and then tucked away in a safe place.

Give each young person a shoebox and markers. Have them decorate their shoeboxes with the markers, making sure they write their name in a prominent place on the box. Ask them to write their name on both the lid and the bottom of the box in case they get separated.

Explain that this activity will be confidential. No one will talk about his or her feelings with anyone else. This is an activity for young people to process their own feelings.

Give each young person five pieces of paper. On each piece of paper, have young people write or draw one upsetting feeling. What makes them mad? Sad? Frustrated? Scared? Lonely? Encourage young people to come up with five upsetting feelings. Remind them again that no one will see what they're putting on their paper.

When young people finish, have them wad up each piece of paper and then step on them and smash them. Encourage them to take out their frustrations on each piece of paper.

Then have young people place these papers into their box to put a "lid on their feelings" for now.

DISCUSSION QUESTIONS

- What did you think of the activity? Why?
- Were five pieces of paper too many? Too few? Why?
- How did it feel to wad up the paper, step on it, and smash it?
- Why is it important to express what you're feeling?
- Why does it matter to not let our feelings overcome us?
- How else can we express our feelings in healthy ways?

BONUS IDEA When young people get wound up, have them each write or draw on one piece of paper about what their feeling. Then have them tear up the paper to symbolize that they're going to get rid of that feeling for now.

Questions Board

FOCUS
Young people ask questions about your group.

SPARKS TIE-IN
- Learning
- Relationships

YOU WILL NEED
- A piece of poster board
- Masking or painter's tape
- A bunch of 3" x 3" sticky notes
- A pencil for each young person

ACTIVITY Display a piece of poster board in front of the group. Give each young person two or three sticky notes and a pencil.

Explain that your group is creating a question board. Encourage young people to write one question they have about your group on one sticky note. They can write as many questions as they wish as long as only one question appears on each sticky note. Ask them not to write their names on the sticky notes.

Questions could be about various topics, such as:

- What your group does.
- A specific skill your group requires.
- Something that will help group members get to know each other better.
- How to improve something within your group.

Give young people time to write a question on a sticky note. When they finish, have them place their sticky notes on the poster board.

When young people finish, choose three to five questions and read them aloud to the group. Encourage group members to answer some of the questions so that the adults aren't the only ones answering the questions.

DISCUSSION QUESTIONS

- Was it hard or easy for you to think of questions? Why?
- How did this activity make you think about our group differently?
- Why is it important to be curious and ask questions?
- What other question topics should we consider?

BONUS IDEA Consider arranging the sticky notes in the shape of a large question mark on the poster board. Or consider using different colors of sticky notes to add some color to the poster board question display.

Around the Circle

84

FOCUS
Young people answer questions about themselves in this circle game.

SPARKS TIE-IN
- Dance/movement
- Family
- Relationships

YOU WILL NEED
- A chair for each young person
- 1 piece of paper for each young person
- 1 pencil for each young person
- A large area

ACTIVITY Create a circle with chairs so that each young person has a chair. Have each young person write his or her first and last names on a piece of paper and place it on a chair. Then have the young person stand behind the chair on the outside of the circle.

Explain that young people will move clockwise around the circle. You will say a series of statements. If the young person can say "yes" to the statement, he or she moves one chair clockwise. If the young person says "no" to the statement, he or she stays in the same place. Thus, there will be times when some chairs don't have anyone standing behind them and other chairs with a line of two to five young people behind them.

The goal of the game is to get around the circle first and back to the chair with your name on it. The first person who does so says, "I made it!" and sits in the chair while the game continues until everyone has made it around the circle.

Here are some sample "yes" and "no" statements to use during this activity:

- You have a brother.
- You are the oldest child in your family.
- You have taken an art class or been in an art club.
- You have a sister.
- Your family owns a car.
- You share a bedroom with another family member.

- You are an only child.
- Your family has moved within the past three years.
- You talk to a grandma or grandpa at least once a week (if not more).
- You were born in another country.
- You usually bring a bag lunch to school.
- Your family has gone camping in the past.
- Your mom has a job.
- You have more than five cousins.
- You play on a sports team.
- You have been to a family reunion.
- You play a musical instrument.
- Your family has a pet.
- You ate dinner with your family last night.
- Your family has a TV.

Play until everyone is seated.

DISCUSSION QUESTIONS

- What did you think of this activity? Why?
- What was it like when you were able to move a lot?
- What was it like when you were stuck behind a chair for a while?
- Why is it important to do different kinds of activities from time to time?
- How else can we take breaks from our usual group activity?

BONUS IDEA Make the game more difficult by having young people move one chair counterclockwise whenever they answer "no" to a statement.

Snowball Blizzard

FOCUS

Young people have a paper snowball fight to get to know each other better.

SPARKS TIE-IN

- Dance/movement
- Relationships

YOU WILL NEED

- A large area
- 3 pieces of 8½" x 11" white paper for each young person
- 1 pencil for each young person

ACTIVITY Give each young person three pieces of paper and a pencil. Have them write one unusual fact about themselves on each piece of paper without putting their name on the paper. For example, one person may write, "I got braces when I was 11" on one piece of paper, "Our family has a pet snake" on another piece of paper, and "My family has traveled to India" on another piece of paper.

When they finish, have them wad up their three papers into three snowball-looking balls of paper and then hold on to them.

Next, have them spread out in a large area. Explain that when you yell, "Snowball blizzard!" they are to start throwing their wads of paper at each other. If a wad of paper falls near them, they can pick it up and throw it at someone else to keep the snowball blizzard going.

Yell, "Snowball blizzard" and let the wads of paper begin to fly. After a few minutes, stop the activity. Have young people sit. Ask them to grab one snowball wad closest to them.

Ask for a volunteer. Have that person open up the paper, read it aloud, and then guess whom it describes. Let them have three guesses. If they don't guess by the third time, have the person who it describes raise his or her hand and say, "That's me."

That person then opens up a snowball and does the same thing. Keep going around the group until all the snowballs have been opened up. (Each young person will do three.)

DISCUSSION QUESTIONS

- How hard or easy was it to come up with three unusual facts about yourself?
- What did you think of the snowball blizzard? Why?
- What one new fact did you learn about a group member today?
- Why is it important to have fun with group members?
- How else can we have fun together?

BONUS IDEA At another time, play the game again. This time have young people write the place they were born on one piece of paper, the name of the school they attended as a kindergarten student on another piece of paper, and the name of their favorite teacher on the third piece of paper.

Guggenheim Earth Puzzle

86

Handout

FOCUS

Help the earth by working on this Guggenheim earth puzzle.

SPARKS TIE-IN

- Advocacy
- Serving, helping, volunteering
- Solving social problems

Our world has many problems, but a lot of people are working to solve these difficulties. Work with a partner to fill in this Guggenheim earth puzzle. Use a thesaurus or dictionary for ideas. See the sample for how to solve this puzzle. Write the name of each animal, place, and problem to solve with a word that corresponds to one of the letters in the word "earth."

	Animal	Place	Problem to Solve
E			
A			
R			
T			
H			

Sample Finished Puzzle

	Animal	Place	Problem to Solve
P	Porcupine	Paris	Pollution
U	Uakari	Uruguay	Unrest
B	Baboon	Bali	Betting
L	Llama	London	Lead
I	Ibis	India	Infections
C	Cat	Colombia	Climate change

Nature Puzzle

87

FOCUS

Find 10 words in this hidden nature puzzle.

SPARKS TIE-IN

- Nature, ecology, environment
- Outdoor life

Look for these 10 words about nature in this word-search puzzle. Circle words as you find them. Cross out the words in the word list after you find each one.

BUSH	CLOUD	GRASS	LEAF	RAIN
PLANT	SEED	SKY	SUN	TREE

L	E	N	I	A	R
T	R	E	E	P	G
S	D	U	O	L	C
S	E	H	R	A	Y
A	E	S	K	N	K
R	S	U	N	T	S
G	O	B	S	H	P
S	U	F	A	E	L

The answer key is found on page 153.

Your Life . . . So Far

FOCUS

Identify the important events of your life up until now.

SPARKS TIE-IN

- Family
- Relationships

Your life has been an adventure. On the lifeline below, write five things that have happened to you since you were born. Maybe you won a contest. Maybe your brother was born. Maybe your family took a great vacation. Maybe your family adopted a pet.

Begin by writing the year you were born on the left-hand end of your lifeline. Then write today's date on the right-hand end of your lifeline. Then add one memorable moment on each of the five lines.

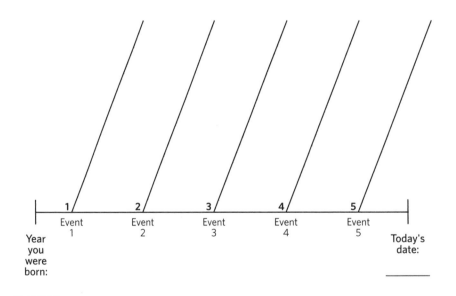

CHAPTER 8

Helping Kids Find Their Sparks Activities

Every child has a spark—or two or three. Each child is interested in some topic or activity and is passionate about it. The problem, however, is that many kids don't know about some of their sparks because they aren't exposed to different interests and activities. They need the chance to try new things and see what interests them and sticks. The activities in this chapter introduce kids to different sparks and help them make sense of what grabs their attention. ▶▶

Spreading Smiles

FOCUS
Young people create smile drawings for the elderly.

SPARKS TIE-IN
- Serving, helping, volunteers
- Solving social problems
- Visual arts

YOU WILL NEED
- 1 copy of the coloring template from the Color A Smile website for each young person (www.colorasmile.org; click on "coloring book")
- 3–5 pieces of 8½" x 11" white paper for each young person
- 3–5 washable markers for each young person

ACTIVITY Explain that many elderly people don't have visitors every day. They don't receive mail every day. Many are lonely. When we color a picture for them, it can brighten their day.

Distribute the coloring template, three to five pieces of blank paper, and three to five markers to each young person. (Young people may want to work at tables in groups so they can share markers to get more of a color variety.)

Have young people decide if they want to draw and color a picture on the blank paper or if they want to color in the picture from the coloring template. Either choice is great.

Once everyone finishes, have the young people show their pictures to the group. Then collect all the pictures. Either distribute them to a nearby nursing home or memory care unit or place them into a nine by twelve inch manila envelope and mail them to Color A Smile (the address is listed on the website).

DISCUSSION QUESTIONS
- What was your first reaction to making pictures for the elderly? Why?
- How do you feel about your artistic capabilities? Why?
- Why does it matter to show our care to the elderly?
- How else can we show our care?

BONUS IDEA Download examples of pictures young people have donated from the Color A Smile website (www.colorasmile.org/masterpieces.html). This often inspires young artists.

Building Rolls

FOCUS
Young people build something new out of empty toilet paper rolls.

SPARKS TIE-IN
- Building and design
- Engineering
- Entrepreneurship
- Solving social problems

YOU WILL NEED
- 1 empty toilet paper roll for each young person
- 3–5 washable markers for each young person

ACTIVITY Give each young person an empty toilet paper roll and some markers.

Explain that millions of empty toilet paper rolls end up in the garbage every year. Instead of throwing them away, we can become creative and reuse them.

Encourage young people to work in small groups to come up with new inventions for their empty toilet paper roll. Talk about how entrepreneurs and engineers develop designs for new products.

If young people are stumped, suggest some of these ideas to get them thinking: an extension cord wrap (to keep extension cords from unraveling), a bird food scoop (when you close one end of the toilet paper roll), a kazoo, plastic bag storage holder for the car (stuff plastic bags inside).

Have young people create their designs. When they finish, have them show their inventions to the group.

DISCUSSION QUESTIONS
- How hard or easy was it for you to come up with ideas for the toilet paper roll? Why?

- Why is it important to reuse items that we otherwise would throw away?
- What other items do we throw away that we could reuse in a new way?
- How else can we care for our environment?

BONUS IDEA Have young people create something new out of a paper towel roll or a wrapping paper roll.

Teaching Others

FOCUS
Young people teach the group something unique.

SPARKS TIE-IN
- Leadership
- Learning
- Teaching/coaching

YOU WILL NEED
- Nothing

ACTIVITY Have young people break into small groups with others they know. Have the small-group members work together to identify the unique talents of each person. (Sometimes young people know more about each other's talents than their own.) Encourage them to think of skills that they can teach the group. Here are some examples: how to whistle with two fingers, secrets to balancing on one foot for a long time, a magic trick, a backward somersault, drawing an animal, asking how you are in another language, making a realistic animal sound, and tips for talking in front of a group without getting nervous.

Once young people have each identified one of their talents, have them take turns teaching them to the group. See how many others can learn these new talents.

DISCUSSION QUESTIONS
- Which is easier: identifying what you're talented at or identifying what someone else is talented at? Why?

- How did it go to teach the group your talent?
- Which talent did you enjoy learning most about? Why?
- Why is it important to teach others what we know?
- How else can we discover each other's talents and skills?

BONUS IDEA Have pairs of young people teach the group something, such as a new game or something else. (You can have them do research to find ideas.) This gives young people the chance to practice leadership and teaching skills while working with another person.

Business Start-Up

FOCUS
Young people identify a new business they'd like to start.

SPARKS TIE-IN
- Entrepreneurship
- Leadership
- Learning
- Speech

YOU WILL NEED
- 1 large sheet of newsprint or other type of large paper for every three to four young people plus 1 large sheet of newsprint to hang in front of the group
- 2 washable markers for every three to four young people plus 1 washable marker for you
- Masking or painter's tape

ACTIVITY Create small groups of three or four young people. Give each group one large sheet of paper and two markers.

Explain that each group will create a new business. Maybe they'll create a new product or a new service. Hang the large sheet of newsprint in front of the group, and write the following questions:

1. What does your business do?
2. What is your business name?

3. Who would you market your product or service to?

4. How would you get the word out about your business?

5. Why do you think your business is needed?

Have groups brainstorm ideas for a business. Once they've decided on a business, have them answer the five questions on their newsprint. When groups finish, have them present their new business to the entire group. If you have time, encourage other young people to ask questions to learn more about the proposed business.

DISCUSSION QUESTIONS

- How easy or hard was it to come up with ideas for a business?
- How did your group decide which idea for a business was best?
- How hard do you think it would be to start a new business? Why?
- Why is it important for new businesses to start?
- How else can we create new ideas?

BONUS IDEA Have each group create a product. Then have them make a prototype of the product to show the entire group.

What You Believe

FOCUS

Young people stand up for their beliefs.

SPARKS TIE-IN

- Advocacy
- Spirituality

YOU WILL NEED

- A large area

ACTIVITY Designate one area of your space as the "yes" side and another area as the "no" side. Have everyone stand.

Explain that you're going to read a statement. Those who agree with it should run to the "yes" side. Those who disagree with the statement should run to the "no" side.

Say, "We are spiritual beings when we are born." Allow time for young people to move to the "yes" or the "no" side of your space. Then have young people notice how many people are on each side. Explain that there is no right or wrong answer.

Then explain you're going to read another statement. Those who agree with it should go to the "yes" area. Those who disagree should go to the "no" area. Some young people will end up moving and some will stay on the same side.

Say, "Once we get older, we decide whether or not to be spiritual beings." Give time for young people to move. Allow them time to notice how many people are on each side.

Read other statements one at a time, giving young people the chance to agree or disagree. Here are some sample statements:

- There is more than one God.
- Religious beliefs create more problems than good.
- My family is spiritual.
- Being religious is different from being spiritual.
- People in my family have different ideas about spirituality.
- We don't know what happens after we die.
- Spirituality is important to me.

DISCUSSION QUESTIONS

- Was it easy or hard to decide how to answer each statement?
- How often do the people around you talk about what they believe in?
- How have the beliefs you had when you were younger changed?
- Why is it important to know what you believe in?
- How else can we discover what we believe in?

BONUS IDEA Get more ideas and information from Search Institute's Center for Spiritual Development at www.search-institute.org/spiritual-development.

Exploring Different Sparks

FOCUS
Young people identify and explore different sparks.

SPARKS TIE-IN
- All of them

YOU WILL NEED
- 18 pieces of 8½" x 11" white paper
- 18 washable markers

ACTIVITY Create nine groups of young people. If you have fewer than 18 young people present, form five groups.

If you have nine groups, give each group two pieces of paper and two markers. If you have five groups, give each group three to four pieces of paper and three to four markers.

Assign each group a different topic. Have them write their topics on one piece of paper. Here are the topics:

1. **Helping others:** Advocacy, serving, helping, volunteering, solving social problems

2. **Animals and nature:** Animals, nature, outdoor life

3. **Building:** Building, design, engineering

4. **Learning:** Computers, learning, reading, teaching

5. **Arts:** Creative arts, drama, theater, music, photography, film, visual arts

6. **Body sparks:** Dance, movement, sports, athletics

7. **Character:** Comedy, entrepreneurship, leadership, living in a specific way, spirituality

8. **People:** Family, relationships

9. **Writing and speech:** Journalism, speech, writing

Have each group brainstorm (and write their ideas on the other piece of paper) of practical ways they could explore or act on those sparks at their age. For example, for the body sparks, a group might list soccer, ballet, gymnastics, square dancing, yoga, and karate.

Give groups time to list as many ideas as they can. Once they finish, have groups present their brainstorm list to the larger group. Discuss how there are many opportunities to explore sparks.

DISCUSSION QUESTIONS

- Which of the nine major spark topics are you most drawn to? Why?
- After this activity, do you feel like you have more opportunities to explore sparks? Why or why not?
- Why is it important to try something new?
- How else can we explore sparks?

BONUS IDEA Invite someone from your local Parks and Recreation Department and Community Education Department to talk about what activities they offer for young people.

Scribble Creations

FOCUS

Young people create works of art out of scribbles.

SPARKS TIE-IN

- Creative arts
- Teaching/coaching
- Visual arts

YOU WILL NEED

- 1 white piece of paper (the bigger the better) for each young person
- 1 pen for each young person

ACTIVITY Give each young person a piece of paper and a pen. Have each young person find a partner. If you have an odd number of group members, pair up with the extra person.

Explain that everyone will create a scribble creation. Have each group decide who will be the leader first. Once they decide, have the leader start scribbling or doodling on the piece of paper while the partner copies the scribbles on his or her own piece of paper. Give pairs about 30 seconds to do this.

After 30 seconds, have pairs switch. The follower now leads and the leader now follows. Give pairs 30 seconds to lead and follow.

When the time is up, explain that each person will now work individually. They are to look at their scribbles and make pictures using part of the scribbles. They may decide they can make one picture or many. Encourage them to be creative. Ideas could include a flower jumping over a horse, a building in flames, or an anteater kissing a hippo.

Give young people time to finish their drawings. Ask for volunteers to show what they've created.

DISCUSSION QUESTIONS
- Which did you like best: being a leader or follower for the project? Why?
- Which did you like best: scribbling or creating pictures from the scribbles? Why?
- Why is it important to create art?
- What else can we do to draw out our imagination?

BONUS IDEA Give young people washable markers to color in their pictures. Or have them connect their scribbles with someone else and create a larger picture from the two.

Career Spot

FOCUS
Young people investigate different careers based on different sparks.

SPARKS TIE-IN
- Computers
- Journalism
- Speech
- All other sparks

YOU WILL NEED
- A computer with Internet access for each young person (or each pair of young people)

- 1 piece of 8½" x 11" white paper for each young person
- 1 pen or pencil for each young person

ACTIVITY Find a bank of computers to use at a school media center, public library, or local organization.

Give each young person a piece of paper and a pen or pencil.

Explain that young people will explore three careers. Have young people go to the Bureau of Labor Statistics website that lists careers for young people. Visit www.bls.gov/k12/azlist.htm. Encourage them to start with the letter that's the same as the first letter of their first name and then work backward or forward from there. (Otherwise most of the careers chosen may end up in the As and Bs.)

Have young people choose two careers that are connected to topics they're interested in. Then have them choose one career that they either haven't heard of before or don't know much about.

Ask them to list the three careers on their piece of paper. Then have them jot down notes about what they learned about each career from the website.

Once everyone finishes, have young people report to the group on one of the careers they investigated.

DISCUSSION QUESTIONS
- Was it easy or hard to find careers that interested you? Why?
- What did you learn that you found interesting?
- Why is it important to explore careers?
- How else can we learn more about careers?

BONUS IDEA Click on "Teacher's Guide" on the Bureau of Labor Statistics website for more information and ideas.

Sparks: Past and Present

FOCUS

Young people remember their former sparks and compare them to the ones they have now.

SPARKS TIE-IN

- Relationships
- Teaching/coaching
- All other sparks

YOU WILL NEED

- Nothing

ACTIVITY Have young people each find a partner. If you have an odd number of people, create one group of three.

Have partners talk about which sparks (interests or activities they love to do) they had when they were preschoolers. Give partners time to talk.

Then have partners discuss which sparks they have now. Give partners time to discuss their interests.

DISCUSSION QUESTIONS

- What were examples of sparks when you were a younger?
- What are examples of sparks that you have today?
- How have your sparks changed over time? Did any stay the same? Which ones?
- Why does it matter to remember which sparks you had in the past?
- How else can we discover our sparks?

BONUS IDEA Do a group tally. How many young people had sparks that stayed the same from when they were younger? How many had sparks that changed?

Adults with Spark

FOCUS
Young people examine adults who act on their sparks.

SPARKS TIE-IN
- Leadership
- Learning
- Teaching/coaching

YOU WILL NEED
- Newsprint or other type of large paper
- 2 washable markers
- Masking or painter's tape

ACTIVITY As a group, identify adults who are acting on their sparks. Adults could include famous people (such as the president of the United States, a famous basketball player, a famous actress, or another newsmaker). Adults also could include people whom kids know personally (such as teachers, coaches, or parents).

Have young people identify an adult and what that person's spark is. Write the name and the spark on newsprint.

DISCUSSION QUESTIONS
- Which sparks are common? Why do you think that is?
- Which sparks are unusual?
- What happens if an adult doesn't have a spark? What is that person like?
- Why does it matter to look up to adults who are acting on their sparks?
- What else can we learn from adults who are acting on their sparks?

BONUS IDEA Research one (or more) of the adult's past interests. What were this person's sparks when he or she was younger?

Your Posters, Your Pictures

FOCUS

See what your posters, pictures, and other images you keep around you reveal about your sparks.

SPARKS TIE-IN

- Creative arts
- Photography/film
- Visual arts

What images do you hang on your bedroom walls? What appears on your computer background screen or on your cell phone? Which photos mean the most to you?

Draw (or write out) three different images you have displayed somewhere in your life that are important to you.

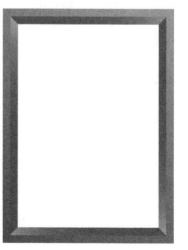

Ask yourself these questions:

- Why do these images mean the most to me?
- What other images do you wish you had in your room?

Discovering Your Sparks

100

Handout

FOCUS

Find out more about your sparks by the actions you take and the interests you have.

SPARKS TIE-IN

- All of them

A spark is something you're interested in, something you love to do. Everyone has at least one spark, if not more.

Answer the following questions in the boxes below to discover more about your sparks.

Which activities do you enjoy doing most? (For example: Sports, clubs, teams, arts, music, drama)

Which subject (or topics) do you enjoy? (For example: Trains, dance, saving endangered species)

If you had a day to choose whatever you wanted to do, what would make you want to jump out of bed?

My Spark, My Goal

FOCUS

Identify one small step you can take to learn more about or practice your spark.

SPARKS TIE-IN

- All of them

Your spark is something you love to do or learn about. Think of your **number 1 spark** as you write about each situation.

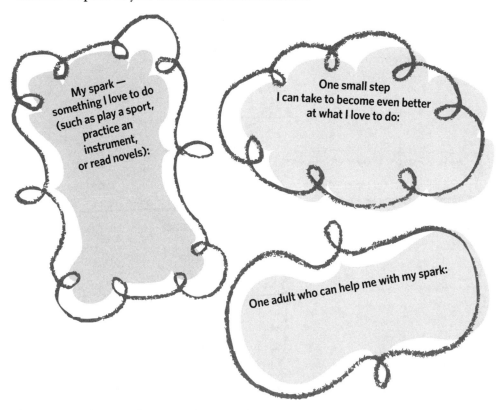

My spark — something I love to do (such as play a sport, practice an instrument, or read novels):

One small step I can take to become even better at what I love to do:

One adult who can help me with my spark:

Learn more about sparks at **www.ignitesparks.org**.

SPARKS INDEX

In *Sparks: How Parents Can Help Ignite the Hidden Strengths of Teenagers*, author Peter L. Benson, PhD, outlines major categories of sparks. The activities in this book tap into these categories, which are in alphabetical order.

TOPICAL INDEX

Answer Key to Puzzle on page 131.

L	E	N	I	A	R
T	R	E	E	P	G
S	D	U	O	L	C
S	E	H	R	A	Y
A	E	S	K	N	K
R	S	U	N	T	S
G	O	B	S	H	P
S	U	F	A	E	L

ABOUT THE AUTHOR

Jolene L. Roehlkepartain is an author, parent educator, and speaker on family and children's issues. She presents workshops to parents, childcare providers, educators, health-care professionals, faith communities, librarians, people in the workplace, and community leaders. She is the author or coauthor of more than 25 books, including *Building Assets Together, Fidget Busters, Parenting Preschoolers with a Purpose, Raising Healthy Children Day by Day,* and *Teaching Kids to Care and Share.* She lives in Minneapolis, Minnesota.